WHOSE ? TREES

A PEOPLE'S VIEW OF FORESTRY AID

SUDAN

MOHAMED AHMED HISHAM

NEPAL

JAN SHARMA

TANZANIA

ANTHONY NGAIZA

WITH

NICHOLAS ATAMPUGRE

Published by Panos Publications Ltd
9 White Lion Street
London N1 9PD, UK

First published 1991
Reprinted 1992

British Library Cataloguing in Publication Data
Whose Trees? A People's View of Forestry Aid
1. Developing countries. Foreign assistance
I. Hisham, Mohamed Ahmed
338.91
ISBN 1 - 870670 - 25 - 6

Funding for *Whose Trees?* was provided by FINNIDA.

Any judgements expressed in this document should not be taken to represent the views of any funding agency. Signed articles do not necessarily reflect the views of Panos or any of its funding agencies.

The Panos Institute is an information and policy studies institute, dedicated to working in partnership with others towards greater public understanding of sustainable development. Panos has offices in Budapest, London, Paris and Washington DC.

For more information about Panos contact:
Juliet Heller, The Panos Institute

Managing editor: Olivia Bennett
Production: Sally O'Leary
Picture research: Adrian Evans
Cover design: Viridian
Cover photograph: Shambu Manandhai
Maps: Philip Davies
Printed in Great Britain by
Ebenezer Baylis, Worcester

All currencies have been converted at the February 1991 rate

Contents

Acknowledgements

Collective effort has been the guiding principle in the writing of this book, and many people in Tanzania, Sudan, Nepal, Finland and Britain were actively involved in its development. The individuals who contributed as members of the evaluation teams are acknowledged at the beginning of each country report. Others whose help has been invaluable include Jon Tinker, Geoff Barnard, Nigel Twose and Heywote Bekele of the Panos Institute in London, Sue Balding, Peri Batliwala, Steve Bristow of SOS Sahel UK and Dr Robert Bensted-Smith.

The following introduction was written by **Nicholas Atampugre,** a Ghanaian consultant/researcher on food security and social transformation issues, who coordinated the research and writing of the three country reports in *Whose Trees?*

The Search for
New Perspectives

As the world moved out of the 1980s, the upheavals in Eastern Europe seemed to promise a decade of hope, hope for greater democracy in the world. Yet 1991 began with war in the Gulf and the threat of environmental pollution on a catastrophic scale. Economic recession seemed to be deepening, and many people in the North were convinced that the world was heading for a major crisis, with soaring unemployment and a decline in living standards.

Meanwhile, millions of people in the Third World, particularly the rural poor, went about their lives as cheerfully as they could. They were baffled by government warnings about the Gulf crisis, global recession and difficult times ahead. Their world has been in crisis for as long as they can remember. Their crisis is one of survival: insufficient and inadequate food for many households and a continuing struggle to meet daily needs for water and fuelwood. Many of the rural poor have learned that to survive they must plan their lives on a day-by-day basis, or according to the annual harvest cycle. The long term must take care of itself.

For more than three decades vast amounts of time, money and talk has been devoted to development aid to the Third World, both from official government sources and private non-governmental organisations (NGOs). Western media and governments have tried to create the impression that all this activity has promoted

Sayed Yasin Mohmood/Panos Pictures

Sole survivor of a once-forested area in Sudan.

development in the recipient countries. Yet the cycle continues: desperate families trying to live off exhausted soils are driven to invade forests or to cultivate marginal lands—thus hastening further environmental decline, poverty and famine. Why has foreign aid had such minimal impact on the lives of rural people?

Part of the reason stems from the concept of development held by many donor agencies. All too often, they assume that development is something they bring to the Third World. In effect, donors impose notions of "progress" coloured by their own history and experience, and believe that by bringing their own perspectives and technology to a recipient country, development will automatically follow.

The beginnings of forestry aid

The history of forestry aid highlights some of the misconceptions and contradictions which have bedevilled the aid industry and compromised its chances of success.

In many countries of Africa and Asia, development assistance to forestry dates back to the colonial era, a century or more ago, when forestry departments were set up: in India by the British and in Tanzania by the Germans, for example. These departments developed as part of a colonial administrative structure and reflected colonial priorities. For example, the forestry department of Ghana, then the Gold Coast, was created in 1908. The primary objective was to facilitate and control the extraction of forest products. By 1925, forest exports, particularly of mahogany, stood at 2,200,000 cubic metres, valued then at UK£286,000 (over UK£5 million or US$10 million at today's prices).

In some countries, controlled harvesting and scientific management techniques were gradually developed, with foresters acting as pioneers in forest conservation and botanical research. Elsewhere, extracting timber at the fastest possible rate remained the simple goal. For the most part, foresters acted as policemen, guarding the national resource from "illegal" exploitation, and as tax collectors, raising revenue from fines and cutting permits. Few colonial foresters saw any connection between forests and the people who lived in, around and off them. Their traditional rights to use the forest and their substantial fund of knowledge about its resources were largely ignored. Local communities were seen at best as a source of labour, at worst as illegal encroachers.

Contradictions

After independence, forestry departments in Africa and Asia inherited much of the infrastructure and attitudes of the colonial offices they replaced, with all their ambiguities and contradictions. There has been an emphasis on creating forest reserves, in order to preserve catchment areas and water supplies and to conserve forest resources. At the same time, there has been continuing pressure to maximise revenue. Foresters have had the often contradictory roles of protectors and exploiters.

The aid which followed immediately after independence was in most countries directed towards institutional development, with a view to increasing forestry's contribution to the national economy. Money, equipment and expertise was aimed at strengthening the capacity of forestry departments to manage forests, to prevent encroachment and expand production. Saw mills, pulp mills and other wood-based industries were also developed. For the forests

Jeremy Hartley/Panos Pictures

The droughts and the energy crisis of the 1970s shifted donors' attention away from commercial exploitation towards forests as a source of fuelwood and a means of combating soil erosion.

and their peoples, little had changed since colonial times.

Local people found themselves dispossessed of "their" forests in the "national interest", losing a resource which was vital to their daily survival. Deprived of their traditional rights to use the forest, many were forced into the role of illegal encroachers, grabbing what they could with no longer any incentive to manage the resource sustainably.

Changing priorities

The energy crisis of the 1970s forced a review of the traditional approach. Suddenly the role of trees as suppliers of fuelwood—an aspect which has always been at the heart of the local communities' perception of forests—attracted global attention. Policymakers in donor and recipient countries alike started to talk about fuelwood, not least because of their desire to reduce urban centres' reliance on imported oil. As a result, the 1970s saw a shift in aid towards meeting the firewood needs of rural communities. The eucalyptus tree took centre stage, and eucalyptus plantations sprang up throughout the Third World, particularly in India.

In the same decade, the Sahelian region of Africa experienced prolonged and extensive drought. As the extent of deforestation in Africa was revealed, international attention was focused on the environmental role of forests. The impact of the drought magnified the difficulties many rural communities were already having in surviving off desiccated and eroded agricultural land. Planting trees was seen as one of the only ways of halting the process of desertification.

By the 1980s the main emphasis of forestry aid was moving away from forests for the nation towards trees for the people. Social forestry, community forestry and agroforestry are different ways of saying much the same thing, and the debate over who should own and benefit from forests has shifted in favour of local communities. Nevertheless, foresters are still bound by their conventional approaches and familiar methods. Many early attempts at community forestry were merely miniature versions of commercial forestry plantations: rows of eucalyptus planted in straight lines and surrounded by fences.

Gerry Foley/Panos Pictures

Eucalyptus plantation in Gujarat, India. Many early attempts at community forestry were merely scaled-down versions of commercial plantations, involving little or no contact with local people.

Nor has forest policy and practice escaped the traditional top-down approach to development: first, identify the priorities of the villagers, then import the "goodies" (from Land-rovers to chain saws) and get the job done. Village communities were not encouraged to feel that they could be masters of their own development.

Many branches

The late 1980s saw yet another shift in forest policy: a move towards an integrated approach which links trees to every aspect of rural life: to food, fodder, fuelwood, health, shelter, education and water. There is increasing recognition, for example, that although the shortage of fuelwood is due to deforestation, the solution does not lie simply in planting trees. Project designers are under pressure to incorporate more effective and extensive participation by local people in the planning process and greater flexibility into implementation.

This change in emphasis has also been brought about by a greater willingness to be self-critical on the part of some policymakers and donors, and by a growing recognition that rural farmers have a great deal of collective knowledge and experience of every aspect of rural life, including trees. If a balance between greater productivity and environmental protection—the goal of sustainable forestry—is to be achieved, policies must take account of and build on local knowledge.

Sustainable forestry is beginning to be the phrase on many a forester's lips, but putting it into practice is not easy. The greatest difficulty facing aid donors is designing forestry projects that really work, especially when public opinion in western countries seeks dramatic solutions to desertification and deforestation. Many different interests need to be reconciled, not least between those who see forests as a source of trees and other products and those who see them as a source of cultivable land. The environmentalist lobby has emphasised protection without room for any exploitation of forest resources, and this has undermined the argument for sustainable use of forest resources.

Forestry departments have had a legacy of mistrust to shake off, and foresters have needed to learn an array of new skills and methods which take account of people, rather than just trees. Such changes in orientation cannot be accomplished quickly.

Finnish forestry aid

FINNIDA (Finnish International Development Agency) was a relative latecomer to the aid business—more as a result of its lack of colonial past than any reluctance to help. Finland's programme of development aid began in 1965 but it was not until the 1980s that development cooperation gained the level of support from the government that the Finnish public had given it. In that decade, the amount of aid flowing from Finland to the developing world grew fast, increasing from just 0.2% of the country's GNP in 1980 to reach 0.63% in 1989.

FINNIDA's long-standing policy has been to concentrate cooperation in those areas where Finland's expertise is well recognised. With two-thirds of the country covered in trees, assistance to the development of forestry has always been a priority. Currently FINNIDA is financing or co-financing over 40 forestry projects in more than 20 countries. During 1989, 16.8% of Finland's bilateral (government to government) aid was channelled to forestry, forest industries and agriculture: US$73 million out of total bilateral aid of US$435 million. Africa has always been the largest recipient of Finnish forestry aid. In 1989 it received 46%, most of which was channelled to the Southern Africa region, while Asia received 20.7%.

FINNIDA's forestry policy reflected domestic experience: the commercial development of forest resources. Its practice of tying aid to the use of Finnish goods and services meant a heavy reliance on Finnish consulting firms, whose experience was overwhelmingly biased towards the extraction of timber and the use of high technology. Finland is a country with a small, stable

Sayed Yasin Mohmood/Panos Pictures

Are donors really addressing the issue of sustainability by introducing expensive imported nursery technology which cannot be maintained when aid packages come to an end?

population, a declining need for farmland, and a vast forest resource. Such conditions are virtually the opposite of those in the developing countries where FINNIDA operates. During the 1980s there was growing criticism that Finnish forestry policy was failing to meet the needs of the Third World.

In 1989 an independent expert group conducted an appraisal of the long-term policy objectives of Finnish aid. It endorsed a continued emphasis on forestry but recommended a flexible approach. FINNIDA's forestry strategy, according to its 1989 *Annual Report*, currently advocates "an integrated approach to forestry development combined with a recognition of the importance of the needs of the rural populations who are directly associated with forests and wood production". As part of the debate over the objectives and orientation of its aid programmes, FINNIDA agreed to the commissioning by the Panos Institute of independent evaluations of three Finnish-assisted forestry projects.

Project evaluations are usually carried out by foreign "experts" on appraisal missions, who rarely talk at length to the rural people whose lives are meant to be improved by the projects. Their terms of reference tend to focus on the stated objectives and technical targets for the period under review. The issue of how far the project meets the priorities of the people is rarely addressed in any depth. *Whose Trees?* takes a different approach. The brief of the Panos evaluation teams was to reflect the views of the people, and three key questions underpinned their research. Who was the project meant to benefit and how? Who is benefiting in practice? What are the local people's views on any benefits?

Policy into practice

The three FINNIDA-sponsored projects studied are the White Nile Rural Forestry Development Project in Sudan, the East Usambara Catchment Forest Project in Tanzania and the Hill Forest Development Project in Nepal. Together, the projects cover a range of geographical conditions and forestry strategies.

Although the first two projects are in Africa, they are located in very different climatic zones and reflect different environmental concerns. In the Sudan project, the main priority is to halt desertification and restore plant cover to a barren region of the country. The primary objective of the Tanzanian project is to halt the growing encroachment on a tropical forest, to preserve the rare species of the area and to stabilise water supplies. The Nepal project concentrates on forest rehabilitation and stems from the need to meet urban fuelwood demands. The emphasis is on forest management and the encouragement of natural regeneration of the hill forests.

All three projects have undergone changes, reflecting past failures, shifts in forestry thinking and the lessons of putting policy into practice.

The aim of the Panos studies was to provide independent overviews of the projects and to examine their impact on the communities as perceived by the inhabitants. It was also important that the final reports should be accessible to the non-expert. Finnish aid stems not just from the government; there is a high level of commitment to and interest in development issues among the general public. There are a considerable number of NGOs involved in development information activities and the large "one percent" movement, through which Finns can devote a percentage of their salary to development, shows the extent of public concern.

The Finnish public has actively questioned the effectiveness of aid. People are keen to know whether living conditions have improved in these societies and whether improvements are likely to be lasting. As far as forestry is concerned, they want to find out whether, for example, fuelwood is now more easily available to the majority. And they want to hear the comments of ordinary people, not just development experts.

The aim of the reports

For the Panos Institute, *Whose Trees?* is part of its programme of encouraging greater participation in the development debate by people of the South, and of giving a stronger voice to those whose lives are directly affected.

The teams that conducted the fieldwork and wrote up the reports were all nationals of the countries concerned. Each team consisted of a representative of a non-governmental organisation (NGO) with an interest in environmental issues, a forestry expert and a journalist. The process of researching the project was seen as a valuable exercise in itself which would enrich the local pool of knowledge in the respective countries. The journalist, who acted as team leader, was responsible for writing up the report. FINNIDA saw and commented on the drafts of the report but the judgements and opinions of the authors have not been adjusted, by Panos or by FINNIDA. This book represents a "customer's view" of development assistance.

One key dilemma emerged as common to each study: how to achieve a balance between environmental sustainability, and social and economic sustainability? In Nepal, the people's desperate need for fuelwood and fodder runs counter to the need to protect the hill forests and allow them time to regenerate. In Sudan, the need to move swiftly in rapidly deteriorating ecological conditions meant that people's involvement was in effect purchased with short-term incentives, rather than through long-term policies which address their social and economic needs. And in Tanzania, as village elder Saleh Omari put it: "You cannot think about 'conserving genetic resources' when you have an empty stomach."

FINNIDA has undeniable expertise in forestry development. It is unhampered by some of the influences constraining the aid policy of other donors, such as a history of colonial involvement. And FINNIDA believed the three projects examined in this book to be among those closest to achieving their development objectives. Yet what this book reveals is that even under such relatively favourable conditions, it remains extremely hard to put the principles behind sustainable forestry into practice.

An elusive goal?

The Sudan White Nile Rural Forestry Development Project highlights the problems inherent in carrying out forestry projects in semi-arid regions. Is it really feasible to talk about sustainable forestry in semi-desert areas, where most tree cover has been destroyed and shifting sand dunes dominate the landscape? The high-tech approach, using advanced nursery technology, for example, does produce quick and impressive results but it reflects an attempt to cure the symptoms rather than the disease. It is clear that such a project has to address human encroachment and land use practices. This entails developing the sustainable management of land resources. Simply growing trees is not a long-term solution.

The Nepal Hill Forest Development Project recognises that careful management of forest resources is the key to halting forest and land degradation. It has proved an innovative and relatively successful approach. Nevertheless, the key issues of land hunger and forest ownership remain unresolved, which has major implications for sustained community participation. The Nepal study also highlights issues related to project planning and implementation. Serious miscalculations in the initial plan caused a radical change of direction and so a substantial waste of time and resources.

The East Usambara Catchment Forest Project in Tanzania represents an interesting shift from exploitation of forest resources to nature conservation. This change was brought about in the 1980s by an international outcry against excessive logging in the Usambaras, partly blamed on FINNIDA support. Nevertheless, the

Clearing forests for timber and land in Zaire. Some developing countries argue that they should be compensated for sacrificing revenue from a natural resource for conservation purposes.

need to protect rare indigenous species will be unrealisable if the focus is on conservation pure and simple; local people are justifiably more concerned with meeting their food and income needs and will continue to be so.

The Tanzanian study also highlighted the dangers of a prolonged gap between the design of a project and its implementation. Such lengthy delays stifle villagers' initiative and willingness to participate, especially when most of the discussion takes place in cities, far away from the forest and its people.

The right to participate

Each of the three projects has highlighted the importance of community involvement if sustainable forestry is to become a realistic goal. People's participation has become the buzzword in development literature and, like many convenient catch-all phrases, it is hard to define. It is easy to analyse why top-down projects fail, but it is much more difficult to identify alternative mechanisms which work.

In practice, the direction and priorities of many projects are determined by a small group: donor agency staff, consultants, local government officials and project workers. During the design stage of a project, people may be asked for information or even for their opinions—but decisions are almost always outside their control. When project staff do take the time to consult local people over the implementation of a project, all too often they do not translate the answers into concrete actions. And very rarely do they ask people what should be done in the first place.

So how can true participation be ensured? One difficulty is that each rural or urban area has its social and economic peculiarities which impose constraints on the form of popular participation. No single strategy will apply everywhere. Perhaps it is better to see popular participation as the overall goal, within which various processes take place. The objective is to ensure that the project is in the interest of the majority of the people and that it will be controlled and directed by them, using individuals and infrastructure accountable to them. The objectives of a participatory strategy need to reflect local priorities, and its driving force should be the motivation of the local people. In practice, solutions will often be specific to individual project areas. Such solutions are only arrived at over time and through experimentation.

While there is no universal recipe, the reports do suggest certain practices which could be incorporated into the design and implementation of any project aiming to facilitate popular participation.

Reaching the people

Involving the local people should start with the recognition that no society is homogeneous. It is important to identify all the interested parties, list their priorities, which may conflict, and link these priorities with the project's objectives in a way that will coincide with the interests of the majority and improve their long-term well-being.

There should be regular meetings and discussions from the planning stages through to implementation. The emphasis should be on learning from local people how best to implement the project, rather than simply informing them of decisions taken or activities to be carried out.

Of great importance is the extent of local people's decision-making powers. They may be ignorant of technical details, but they know what is in their interest. To regard them as a passive "target group" is to put them at the periphery of the project's activities. Broad participation means that the local community is actively involved in the main components of the project and in finding solutions to problems. Issues such as budget allocation for specific activities should not be the preserve of a few bureaucrats.

As the Sudan report shows, it is vital to establish clearly the basis for motivation. Is the community's involvement to be based on individual material advantage, indirect benefits such as increased social services or improved infrastructure, or even non-material advantage such as the prestige of being part of a well-funded project? The experience of the Sudan project shows that it is dangerous to use cash or goods as the sole incentives for motivation. This may produce an initial burst of enthusiasm, but with no solid basis the commitment may falter and evaporate. For sustained motivation, the benefits must be genuine, tangible and long-lasting.

A fresh perspective

Few donor agencies will voluntarily subject their funding policy and practice to independent scrutiny. These studies of FINNIDA's work will, we hope, influence the way future forestry projects are implemented. Some of the problems identified—such as delays and inadequacies in project planning—can be addressed by donors. Others, such as inappropriate national policies, can only be dealt with by the recipient governments.

But as well as examining past mistakes, the reports provide a fresh perspective on forestry development—that of the local men and women whose lives are directly affected and who have for too long remained on the periphery of project design and development. One Tanzanian villager had a weary comment on plans to mobilise local support in the Usambaras: "Will they abandon the project if we think that it is against our interests?"

Whose Trees? demonstrates that there are no simple solutions to environmental degradation. There are invariably conflicts of interest between local people, governments and donor agencies. These will never be satisfactorily resolved unless there is a willingness and an ability to continually scrutinise and question development projects. This has to be undertaken by national governments and donor agencies. More importantly, local people also need to have the power to critically question the relevance of foreign aid to their daily lives. No amount of consultancies can replace grassroots opinions. One Tanzanian villager, Hamza Athmani, commented on a forestry official whose work with the local community has been conspicuously successful: "This man succeeded because he came to my people as someone needing to learn from them. The problem with many others who had come before him is that they came to us as philosopher kings."

The White Nile Rural Forestry Development Project, Sudan

This report was written by **Mohamed Ahmed Hisham,** a freelance journalist based in Khartoum. He was assisted by **Izat Mirghani,** chairman of The Environmentalist Society in Khartoum; **Dr Salah Goda Hussein,** head of the department of forestry, University of Khartoum; **Eiman El Rasheed Eltyeb,** an MSc student in the department of forestry, who examined women's involvement; and **Sayed Yasin Mohmood,** photographer.

Disappearing Trees and Mobile Dunes

Fathi el Fadl struggled to find the gears as he drove his rickety Toyota through the dusty side streets of Khartoum. He pointed ahead, beyond some buildings. "There, my son, is where I used to hunt. All over there was forest and plenty of animals." Fathi has been a taxi driver for 45 years and knows every corner of the city. "I can't believe my eyes," he said. "All the trees and animals which surrounded the city seem to have vanished overnight, replaced by buildings and dust."

As he spoke, the sky turned grey, and he shook his head, anticipating yet another of Khartoum's familiar dust clouds. In the remaining rural areas around the city and in nearby villages unprotected by tree cover, years of these dust clouds have transformed fertile fields into acres of worthless sand.

Fathi's frustration at this rapid environmental decline is shared by millions of Sudanese throughout the country. But many rural farmers do not even have the option open to Fathi. He has been able to stick it out in Khartoum, earning a living by ferrying the capital's numerous visitors around the city.

Driving south to Kosti on a hot sunny day in the long dry season, the flat, barren landscape stretches endlessly ahead. There is an occasional shrub, a dry twig or a few goats, but all that seems to flourish are roadside coffee tables, loaded with Pepsi Cola for thirsty travellers.

It was not always like this. The people of Kosti can remember losing their way in the dense vegetation as they walked from one village to another. They can also recall the rich variety of trees. One older villager could name 18 tree or shrub species, and told of villages called after certain tree species—the village of Bobnis comes from "ebonis", the blackwood tree (*Dalbergia melanoxylon*). Most of these tree species have vanished, leaving many such villages marooned in a dusty and dry landscape, their people forced to eke out a living without forest resources. Once animals roamed the villages, providing an important source of food. These animals have disappeared along with the vegetation, leaving only domestic livestock.

Yet the picture is not entirely bleak. Around Tendelti the remnants of forests, or at least of tree and bush cover, are still visible. The sand dunes have not yet spread up to the northeast, where the Beni Gerrar people live, about 65 km from Tendelti. Here it is possible to strengthen and improve the remaining natural forest.

The White Nile Rural Forestry Development Project, supported by FINNIDA, aims to turn the tide against the mobile sand dunes and restore the forests, to provide not just vegetation cover but also trees from which the local people can derive some income. It plans to restore to the area the once flourishing gum arabic tree (*Acacia senegal*), a low thorn tree, the resin of which produces a valuable gum.

The Sudan-Finland forestry programme

The White Nile project is one of six schemes being run under the Sudan-Finland forestry programme, which is the largest externally funded forestry programme in the country. It was drawn up by the Sudanese and Finnish governments and launched in 1979. Under the agreement, Finnish consultants advise on forestry and forest industries. The main objectives are to prevent the process of desertification and, through afforestation, to protect the arable land against harsh, drying winds and drifting sand dunes. In the long term this should result in increased local food production and improved living conditions by returning land to cultivation.

The government of Sudan was particularly keen to restore the gum arabic tree, known locally as *hashab*, to its natural regions of growth, such as the White Nile province. Gum arabic is used in the manufacture of pharmaceuticals and confectionery and in photography, lithography and food processing, and is the country's third biggest export earner: US$75 million in 1988/89 according to

---

Finland's assistance to Sudan's forestry sector:

- Support to the Forestry Technicians Division of the Khartoum Polytechnic at Soba.
- Institutional support to the Forests National Corporation (FNC) Headquarters, Khartoum.
- Support to the Forestry Research Centre at Wad Medani.
- Rehabilitation and management of Sunt and Upland Forests in the Central region.
- Khartoum Greenbelt Rehabilitation and Afforestation on farmlands and support to fuelwood plantations in the Rahad area.
- The White Nile Rural Forestry Development Project. This project, the subject of this study, focuses on combating desertification through developing plantations of mesquite (*Prosopis chilensis*), a drought-resistant tree, and the promotion of gum arabic production by encouraging widespread replanting of *Acacia senegal*, known in Sudan as *hashab*.

Finnish government assistance is normally channelled through Finnish consultancy companies, such as Enso Forest Development Ltd, which have considerable experience in forestry and forest-related industries.

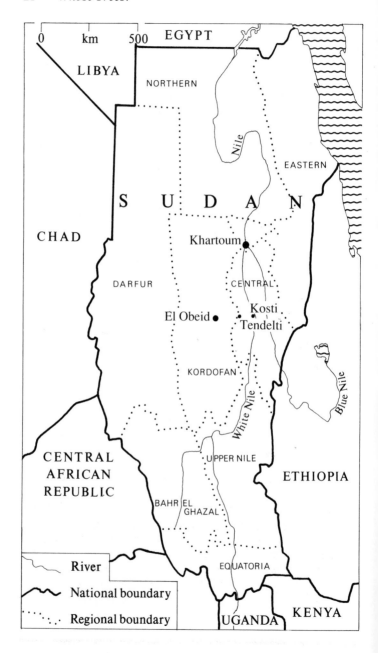

the World Bank. Although manufacturers have been turning increasingly to substitutes, there is still a world market and the tree has the potential to increase Sudan's foreign exchange earnings.

The White Nile Rural Forestry Development Project

The White Nile project is centred around the Kosti and Tendelti areas and is being carried out in five stages. The first (1979-80) was a preparatory phase investigating methods of producing seedlings and planting efficiency. This is important because of the extremely short Sudanese planting season, normally between mid-July and mid-August. During the second phase (1981-82) a nursery was set up in Um Hager (15 km south of Tendelti) to produce an average of half a million seedlings a year. Trials were carried out growing mesquite *(Prosopis chilensis),* the drought-resistant tree which it is hoped will halt the movement of the sand dunes because of its ability to tolerate extremely arid conditions and trap wind-blown sand. Another trial planted *hashab* (gum arabic) seedlings, which it was hoped would become a valuable source of income for village farmers.

The third phase (1983-85) was primarily one of evaluation. The 1985 report—while noting that considerable losses had been incurred due to the exceptional drought of 1984, as well as from grazing by animals—found "ample evidence to show that in years of above normal rainfall, if properly protected against animals, plantations succeed quite satisfactorily". It recommended that afforestation programmes continue.

Significant Dates: White Nile Rural Forestry Development Project

1979-80: Launching of the Sudan-Finland forestry programme.
Investigation of seedling production and planting methods.
1981-82: Development of nursery component.
1983-85: Trial afforestation.
1986-88: Expansion of afforestation,training and extension work.
1989-93: Expansion of the afforestation programme, with the focus on White Nile province.

During the fourth phase (1986-88), afforestation work was extended: new *hashab* plantations were established, and mesquite plantations extended to the northern parts of the Tendelti area. By 1989, the project was ready for the fifth and final stage—which represents a shift from afforestation alone to a more integrated forestry programme at village level.

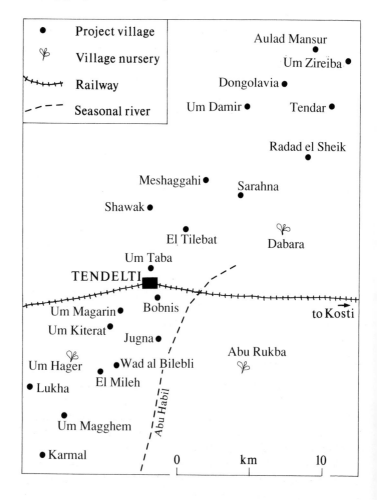

Phase five: 1989-93

This last phase of the project aims to "focus on seedling production, agroforestry, compound planting, school nurseries, improved woodstoves, and natural forest management". It will create a system of satellite nurseries in villages more than 25 km from the central ones, which will help decentralise the afforestation work. These new nurseries will employ paid workers and use local materials.

An important objective is to strengthen the Forests National Corporation (FNC)—the Sudanese Ministry of Forestry—so that it can take over and run the central and satellite nurseries before the end of the project in 1993. Under the project, the FNC will help improve forest management in several areas of the White Nile province where forests are being overexploited, identifying key natural forest areas and appointing staff to help local people draw up management plans. Two forest areas in Kosti and Tendelti have been selected for study by the FNC.

During the project, the central nursery seedling production target is 870,000 a year (370,000 for Kosti and 500,000 for Tendelti) while four pilot satellite nurseries are aiming to produce 15,000 seedlings each a year. As well as mesquite and *hashab* seedlings, fruit trees such as guava and citrus will also be supplied, as villagers prefer them to shade and ornamental trees.

The FNC and its agencies are responsible for the initiatives which are being carried out with the help of the Finnish staff—two specialists in forest management and extension work, a mechanics instructor and a seasonal machinery specialist.

Project history

The project is centred around the two major towns of Kosti and Tendelti and their surrounding villages, in the semi-desert of the White Nile province. In the north of the Tendelti area there are huge arid areas which until now have received no serious attention from development agencies other than FINNIDA. This northern part of the Tendelti area is characterised by vast stretches of sand dunes, known locally as *quz*, some rising as high as 20 metres. Near Kosti, there are gullies filled with swamp deposits from the rains, sand ridges and fixed sand dunes. Yet these areas once formed part of the important gum arabic tree belt, a green and productive region in stark contrast to today's barren landscape.

About 60,000 nomads roam the area tending cattle, but the bulk of the population, some 360,000, are sedentary farmers who rely on the land for their livelihood. Villages vary in size according to the availability of water and other natural resources.

Initial suspicions

At first, local villagers opposed the project, suspicious that the government was plotting to take over their land once it was afforested. It seemed to them that the activities being introduced were like farming, but with trees rather than, say, millet. Yet for them, a tree was a product of nature. The idea of planting one and then waiting years for it to grow before benefiting was at odds with their traditional way of thinking. They reasoned that if they were being asked to plant trees, it could only be to benefit the government.

Attempts were made to persuade the villagers of the benefits to them. Workers visited influential village personalities and gave talks to the local people about the objectives of the afforestation programme. Gazi Khider, an extension officer, explains: "The emphasis is on building up confidence and credibility, which are essential elements in any future relationship between the project and the farmers. What cannot be achieved or will not be done, should not be promised. The acceptance of the idea of planting trees depends on the farmers' commitment to the project objectives."

These early attempts failed to win over the local people. In the rural areas, people look up to their local chiefs, and it was clear that support from these traditional authorities was crucial.

One of the most influential chiefs was El Sherif Meki Aasakir of the Gimaa people of the Tendelti area. When the project staff approached him, he not only welcomed them but also offered part of his own land for a *hashab* plantation. Sudanese foresters believe his help has been instrumental to the project's development.

Nubawi, leader of the Beni Gerrar nomads north of Tendelti, also played a significant role in persuading villagers and farmers to accept the afforestation plan. Like Aasakir, he offered part of his land in the village of Um Zireiba for mesquite planting, and today the tree flourishes in large areas of this otherwise desert region.

Group discussions and slide shows gradually helped dispel initial suspicions and attract farmers to the project. They also provided the extension team with practical ideas on how to organise farmers and to identify the genuinely committed. Village leaders and local teachers also helped convince people to accept the project plans.

The participation of the villagers, initially dependent on endorsement by key village personalities, developed into structured village committees. These were set up after consultation between the extension officer, local chiefs and other influential people. The committee helps the extension worker identify reliable farmers to join the afforestation programme, controls seedling distribution to a network of farmers, supervises exploitation of community forests, and passes on information and advice to the community.

Women were recruited as extension officers, and by phase five extension programmes directed specifically at women's groups had begun. These initially have to work through local chiefs and then male villagers judged to be receptive. Even so, the latter's first response is usually negative, since they often claim that project activities are "men's affairs".

In 1986, the project expanded to the Kosti area, beginning with the rehabilitation of the local tree nursery and the launching of the afforestation programme in neighbouring villages, which were supplied with *Acacia senegal* seedlings. This was backed up by a public education programme designed to promote the aims and objectives of the afforestation activities.

A hot-house approach

Readily available seedlings are crucial to the success of any afforestation programme, and these depend on efficient nursery systems. The nursery system designed by Enso, the Finnish implementing agency, uses greenhouses, plastic shading nets, water pumps, sprinklers and plastic pot trays to achieve impressive production rates. The seeds are treated to assist germination.

The Tendelti central nursery began seedling production in 1982 and the second nursery, at Kosti, started production in 1987. Throughout the project, there have been frequent studies of the nursery and field establishment techniques, with the intention of recommending practices for routine work in the field. In 1988, a FINNIDA appraisal criticised the nursery system as unsuitable for Sudanese conditions because the high proportion of imported components raised the average cost of seedlings. All *hashab* seedlings are now grown in polythene tubes, which are locally available.

By July 1990, there were 660,000 seedlings ready for planting at the Tendelti nursery and 680,000 at Kosti (which produced double its original target). The 1991 production target is 750,000 seedlings per nursery. Targets have been raised to respond to the increasing demands for tree planting in private farms, around households and in village woodlots.

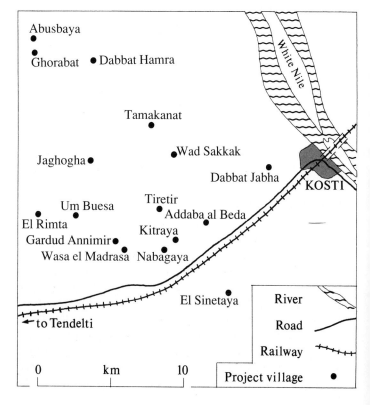

Production figures for the two central nurseries

Um Hager	hashab	1982-89	2,670,000
(Tendelti)	mesquite	1982-89	1,513,900
	others	1987-89	68,700
Total			4,252,600
Kosti	hashab	1987-89	728,000
	mesquite	"	239,700
	others	"	175,600
Total			1,143,300

Women provide a reliable labour force at the central nurseries, particularly at Kosti, and stay longer than most male employees. Much of the work offered by the project is casual, so the relative insecurity and low wages encourage many men to abandon nursery work after gaining some experience. They can migrate and seek better jobs elsewhere; women have fewer employment options.

The satellite nurseries have been hampered by a lack of water, delays in the delivery of materials for building wells and a lack of technical knowledge on the raising of seedlings. Despite this, Tendelti's village nurseries did produce 28,900 *hashab* seedlings in 1987-89, which equals about 1% of the total produced at Um Hager.

"Flying" nurseries

Before the seedlings are transferred to the planting site, nursery staff harden them up by removing their shade and reducing irrigation. Without this, many would not even survive the journey to the planting sites. The seedlings are then packed into trays and carried by truck or tractor to the field. In Kosti, "flying" nurseries are prepared near water sources, around the time of the first rains.

When the rainy season begins, tractors loaded with mesquite seedlings are driven around the villages, and pot trays of 45 seedlings are handed out to households for planting. Private land has been given to the project to be developed into woodlots for the benefit of the whole community and several families share each lot.

Sayed Yasin Mohmood/Panos Pictures

Women provide much of the labour at the project nurseries; men tend to migrate for better paid work.

The farmers and their families plant the seedlings manually. In some cases, they use hired labour since seedlings must be planted quickly during the short rainy season. Mechanical planting by tractor is used only for mesquite in areas of desertification.

Early surveys of the project found that the northern part of Tendelti, where rainfall levels can sometimes drop to as low as 150 mm per year, was severely degraded. It was decided to plant the area with mesquite to help fix the moving sand. South of the Tendelti railway line, the land is less degraded and retains some old gum arabic trees. There, more *hashab* was planted in an effort to restock the gum arabic belt. *Hashab* seedlings were distributed to selected villagers for planting on private land in areas where the conditions were promising.

Later, mesquite seedlings were also distributed for village plantations in areas where rainfall is less and sand encroachment threatens village land. Mesquite has proved a success in most of the areas planted after 1985. Mechanical planting enabled the afforestation teams to complete planting well within the short rainy season. Some 30 villages have been covered so far, involving some 300 farmers.

During the trial planting of *hashab* in 1981-82, each farmer was supplied with 1,000 seedlings every season. The extension team camped at villages during the planting period to demonstrate planting methods, and later to check that the seedlings were being weeded. The workers also maintained a progress report and recorded survival rates.

Total afforested areas in Tendelti and Kosti

Tendelti		
1982-89	3,960 ha	hashab
1982-89	1,671 ha	mesquite
1987-89	58 ha	other species
Kosti		
1987-89	932 ha	hashab
1987-89	105 ha	mesquite
1987-89	25 ha	other species

The earlier plantations failed not only because of the severe drought of 1983 and 1984, but also because of the inexperience of the farmers. The successful plantations are those planted from 1985. The proportion of seedlings which survive the farming season during which they were planted now exceeds 80%. Some plantations are already being used. Gum arabic trees are being tapped. Farmers use a long stick with an iron edge to carve out a scar on the tree stem. The gum that flows out is then allowed to solidify before collection. Thinning and pruning of mesquite trees is also producing firewood and poles for building.

Agroforestry

By 1990, 68 villages were involved in the agroforestry scheme. The project distributed *hashab* seedlings and encouraged farmers to grow traditional seasonal crops such as sesame, watermelon and cucumber alongside them. Millet and sorghum, which tend to suppress *hashab* seedlings, were discouraged but there was enough uncultivated land to provide alternative plots for these staples. Farmers are encouraged to continue cultivating other cash crops such as sesame and groundnuts on these fields until the fifth year, when the *hashab* tree should be mature enough for tapping and so provide income. The idea is that this way farmers can maximise the returns from their fields. In most cases, there is no shortage of land. The limiting factors are shortages of rainfall and labour.

Most farmers agree that as long as the fields are weeded, the yields increase under *hashab* trees because of their nitrogen-fixing quality, which improves the soil. But in practice, it is hard to prove that the increases are due to intercropping, and one or two seasons is too short a time to properly assess the effect.

Intercropping with mesquite is less popular. Most farmers are reluctant to grow crops between the trees, claiming that mesquite creates too much shade and suppresses the crops. So the land given over to mesquite woodlots is not usually needed for cultivation. Where mesquite has been planted alongside food crops, harvesting was only possible during the first season after planting. After that the thorny mesquite trees closed canopy, largely because project staff had planted them mechanically and at closer intervals than *hashab* seedlings. Thinning and/or singling—leaving only the best

Sayed Yasin Mohmood/Panos Pictures

Tapping gum arabic. Low producer prices may force some farmers to cut trees for firewood and replace them with more profitable crops.

stems to grow—should allow the continued cultivation of agricultural crops. A trial in one village, Tendar, has singled out and thinned the mesquite trees, and sesame has been grown between them. The result has been encouraging, giving higher sesame yields under mesquite than in the open.

Collectors and consumers: women's involvement

Women are the chief collectors and users of fuelwood so their involvement in the project, which only effectively began in phase five, is vital for its success. The steady erosion of forest resources has made their burden of meeting household needs even more time-consuming.

The woodstove programme aims to maximise the heat obtained from wood and so to minimise waste in fuel consumption. This is crucial if pressure on the limited forest resources is to be reduced. Women are spending increasing amounts of time, money and energy obtaining the household's fuel needs—between one and four hours a day is usually required to gather firewood. In villages too far away from forests, women have to buy bundles of fuelwood, costing 10 Sudanese pounds (S£)—about US$2—in the Tendelti area and S£15 (US$3) in the Kosti area.

In villages such as Um Damir in Tendelti and Wad Sakkak in Kosti, where there is no fuelwood, women pay S£50 (US$11) for a sack of charcoal. This lasts them about 10 days. In conditions of acute shortage, families resort to using cow dung as fuel. But as Nafissa, a woman farmer of Dabbat Hamra village in the Kosti area explained, the smoke produced is such that "I would go blind using this animal dung continuously as fuel."

In the Kosti area, most women rely on traders to supply their fuelwood needs. Local women were unanimous in their view that charcoal is better than firewood, as it is easier to use and produces less smoke. Recently woodstoves have been introduced into the area. So far, 130 have been built in Ghorabat by village girls trained by extension workers. A further 140 stoves have been built in Wasa el Madrasa and another 122 in Wad Sakkak. In the Tendelti area, 51 stoves have been built in Lukha and 11 in Um Zireiba, the small

Sayed Yasin Mohmood/Panos Pictures

Women are primarily responsible for the collection of firewood. They are directly affected by the scarcity of supplies but their involvement in the project has been limited.

numbers reflecting the lack of water and suitable clay. Despite such constraints, the woodstove programme has made some progress as local women are enthusiastic about using them.

Afforestation

During the dry season, many men migrate to earn money and only the old men, women and children are left behind in the villages. This seasonal phenomenon has placed a heavy burden on women in rural areas. With successive poor harvests encouraging widespread migration, women's role in agricultural production has increased.

Village women participate in all agricultural activities, including land preparation, planting, weeding and harvesting. Most married women participate in cultivation during the rainy season and already possess the minimum knowledge required for involvement in afforestation and agroforestry. In Lukha village, Tendelti area, three women farmers are directly involved in the afforestation programme. Each was given 1,000 *hashab* seedlings to be planted with their seasonal crops.

The women tend to prefer working alone on their own fields, which are usually smaller than those of men, particularly when growing cash crops. Women farmers who take part in the afforestation programme are those who own land, mainly through the Islamic law of inheritance. Women in the villages of Shawak,

Mesquite survives well in harsh conditions, fixing sandy soils and providing fuel and fodder. Its disadvantages are its vicious thorns and its tendency to overwhelm other species.

Jugna and Wad al Bilebli, in the Tendelti area, preferred to share cultivation with fathers or brothers rather than husbands, to avoid what they describe as "trouble". Yet when they harvest their cash crop, they are often compelled to allow their husbands to sell it, since women are barred from selling in the market. Women usually spend their income on domestic items and clothing, while men spend theirs on food. Apart from some cash crop cultivation, most women do not take part in income-generating activities.

At Um Zireiba, in the Tendelti area, the women believe that the mesquite trees have halted the sand drift by providing barriers against, and protection from, wind-driven sand. The trees also provide shade from the heat. Opinions were divided on the impact of agroforestry on land productivity and crop yields. Fatima, of Um Magarin village in the Tendelti area, believed the recent crop yields were related to rainfall levels rather than to intercropping.

The impact of the project

The project has demonstrated that the mesquite tree is an effective survivor. Not only has it withstood the semi-desert conditions, but it has also turned green a number of previously brown and degraded areas.

Mesquite magic

Most farmers know that the loss of top soil reduces the fertility of the land and can drastically affect food production. And those who live in arid conditions know what it means to be without forest protection against hot and dusty winds. The villagers of Um Zireiba are pleased with their mesquite forest. They say the effect of the dust storms are less severe because the forest affords protection. They welcome the shade it gives their domestic livestock—mainly goats, sheep and cattle—and the fodder provided by the mesquite leaves and pods. One farmer even said that his goats gave more milk when fed on mesquite pods.

In Um Damir there are three mesquite plantations. Trees provide shelter for two sides of the village, reducing the impact of the severe winds. Mesquite has been used for a fence around the village school, and the piles of sand trapped behind the trees proves their efficacy.

Ibrahim runs a small food kiosk for travellers who stop at Um Damir on their way to and from Kosti and on towards El Obeid. He calls the mesquite forest "an oasis in the middle of the desert". The strong winds which carried with them a lot of dirt and dust have been reduced, and the domestic livestock which once roamed around his shop, scrounging for food, have now found refuge in the forest. The pods, fallen leaves and lower branches of mesquite make good fodder for grazing animals. And Ibrahim now has a ready supply of fuelwood.

In Dabbat Baida, just outside Kosti, the 900 villagers are mostly animal owners who practise little agriculture. The village lies in front of a sand dune which towers over it on two sides. Mesquite has been planted along the inside of the sand dune. One villager, Mohammed, pointed out some benefits. One year the fence around his house was destroyed by the moving sand and he had to build another mud wall. "Now, 'el hamdo lella' (thank God), the establishment of this shelterbelt has slowed down the movement of sand towards the village. Our animals have found shade and fodder, and we can cut firewood when the project officials allow us."

But the mesquite tree's magical properties have their limits. One of its drawbacks is its capacity to swamp other species as it regenerates. In the irrigated areas of the New Halfa cotton project in Kassala province (eastern Sudan) and the Gezira cotton scheme (Central region), the mesquite tree is regarded as a weed—unwanted and difficult to control. Initially it was used for fencing. But animals feeding on its pods stimulated its rapid regeneration, their digestive systems acting like a nursery pre-treatment. Because it is drought resistant, there is a danger that mesquite might suppress or replace other more productive but less tenacious indigenous varieties. In a natural, diverse forest, there would be a mixture of trees with different qualities—medicinal, herbal, practical, edible, soil-enriching and so on—whereas the value of mesquite, though considerable, is limited.

Tendelti project officials maintain that the chance of mesquite dominating all other species is small. The regeneration process depends on adequate organic matter as well as moisture, but mesquite is being planted around dunes composed of nearly 90% bare sand. Seeds spread by animal defecation are unlikely to

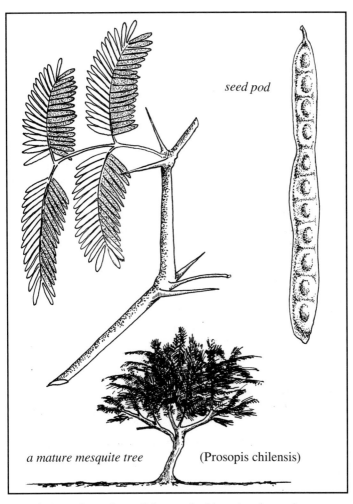

seed pod

a mature mesquite tree   (Prosopis chilensis)

germinate under such conditions and with such a short rainy season.
Even if it did happen, they say, it would be a considerable
achievement, since the project's mesquite covers only about 1,800
hectares of a vast and degraded region.

Another problem with mesquite is the density of the woodlots,
which hinders agroforestry. Eventually, no-one will be able to enter
the forests because of the mesquite's sharp thorns, described by one
villager in Um Zireiba as "nails". Some villagers have complained

that mesquite is poisonous, perhaps because they have developed tetanus infections after thorns have pierced their bare feet. Steve Bristow of SOS Sahel, a British NGO which also runs afforestation projects in Sudan, acknowledges that mesquite thorns are vicious and that farmers are reluctant to work in or near the trees. Thinning or pruning is thus a difficult job, and although cutting back selected areas is perhaps the easiest option, there is always the risk of killing the trees. In his opinion, although its nitrogen-fixing capacity allows it to be grown in impoverished soils, this advantage must be weighed against the difficulty of working with or near it. It is most suited to sites where it does not need much attention and is used primarily for soil conservation or sand stabilisation.

Balla Musa, Tendelti extension officer, explained why the mesquite plantation in Um Damir had become so thick. When the project first planted the area, poor rainfall meant the mesquite seedlings did not shoot up. People thought the seedlings had died and they replanted. When the rains improved, both old and new seedlings picked up and started growing. In addition, the spacing in some areas was incorrect. As a rule, four metres between trees is adequate. But the man operating the planting machine worked inconsistently, sometimes too fast and sometimes too slow, so the plant cover in some areas turned out sparse while in others it proved too dense. Steve Bristow warns, however, that mesquite has the capacity to close canopy even when it is correctly spaced.

Thinning the forest also requires a labour force, something that most farmers cannot afford. Trials are under way to find the best way to thin mesquite, either by pruning the side branches or by removing whole trees and leaving the best ones intact. However, although extension workers offer advice on proper thinning and agroforestry, some farmers find this inhibiting rather than helpful. Abdalla of Um Damir village explained that it made them reluctant to act on their own initiative because they feel the trees are the responsibility of the project.

It is clear that the farmers appreciate the income they can earn from selling fuelwood more than any of the less tangible benefits gained from soil improvement. The owner of a demonstration plantation in Tendelti was apparently not convinced that mesquite did improve the land; he said that his sesame harvest from that plantation was poor.

Despite all these queries and doubts about the advisability of overconcentration on mesquite, at the end of 1990 plantations of the species were well established throughout the north of Tendelti area.

The decline of hashab

The project's original priority was to restore the gum arabic belt, lost as a result of overexploitation and unfavourable weather. The tree has also been a victim of the falling price of gum arabic, which removed the incentive for families to grow it. Its primary importance was as a cash crop with a world market. But this source of income began to decline when prices fell during the 1970s. Meanwhile the price of sesame and groundnut crops continued to increase. Farmers virtually stopped tapping gum arabic in the early 1970s, and now sesame and groundnut have replaced *hashab* as the major source of income. Producer prices, fixed by the government, have not been raised since 1987-88. Gum arabic sales now account for only 10% of farm incomes in the areas where the tree grows, compared with 50% in the 1950s.

Farmers also changed from traditional shifting cultivation patterns to the large-scale planting of cash crops. Medani Ali, an 80-year-old farmer of Wad al Bilebli village, Tendelti area, recalls that "most of the *hashab* trees in this area were cut down in the '60s and '70s to allow cash crops such as groundnuts to be grown." But by clearing large areas of trees, farmers exposed the soil to erosion. Fertility decreased and the cash crop yields also declined.

Professor Abdel Nour, FNC general manager, does not believe that falling gum arabic prices will threaten the planned *hashab* plantations, saying that *Acacia senegal* is not grown for gum alone. "It produces wood and has indirect benefits as it stabilises soils and improves environmental conditions."

Mohammed Ibrahim, a farmer in El Mileh village in the Tendelti area, can remember the days when *hashab* was a lucrative crop. "We used to tap the trees every 10 days....Since 1984, new *hashab* plantations have been planted as a result of the project....I started tapping in January 1989 but the productivity was very low." He is unsure whether drought or tree locusts were to blame. "Soon after,

I left the village. There was no-one else in the family able to continue tapping," he says.

But one farmer, at least, claims benefits from the project plantation. Ahmed Fadil, an 80-year-old villager from Shawak, north of Tendelti, says he collected about 9 kg of gum in 10 days.The producer price in 1989 was over S£9 per kg (about U$2). "If the trees had been protected from the animals and from birds, the yield could have been better," he says. "Another limiting factor is that I did all the tapping alone. My son is no longer here, having, like most young people, emigrated to look for work outside the village."

Labour constraints

Harvesting gum arabic is labour intensive. The increasing dry season migration has affected the productivity of the *hashab* trees. Tapping starts in January and February—the months when most farmers migrate to seek wage labour. And the younger people have not yet mastered the skill of tapping the tree so that it is continuously productive. The lack of a skilled labour force could be an obstacle to the expansion of the gum arabic economy, even where farmers are sufficiently motivated to plant and protect *hashab* trees. Yousif Hussein, one of the younger generation of farmers, lives in the village of Dabbat Baida, Kosti area. He believes that "protecting the trees for four or five years could become problematic, especially if [gum] yields continue to decline, unless farmers are to receive continuous aid."

By July 1990, no significant yield of gum arabic had been obtained from project-planted *hashab* or from natural *hashab* plantations in the project area. The real economic value of the tree, and its impact on these communities, cannot be properly assessed for at least five years. Although yields vary according to rainfall and soil types, the tapping of gum usually starts after five years and continues for about 15 with peak yields occurring between the eighth and tenth years.

Farmers are divided on whether agroforestry is feasible on *hashab* plantations. Most agree that it is possible but that it will depend on how the fields are cultivated. Agricultural crops such as sesame and groundnuts generally do well when grown with *hashab*. Millet and sorghum tend to hinder its growth. One woman farmer,

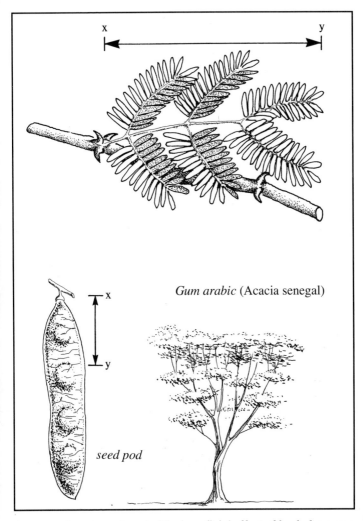

Gum arabic (Acacia senegal)

seed pod

however, is not convinced of the beneficial effect of *hashab* on crop yields. She believes *hashab* is more important in halting the movement of sand dunes.

Hashab plantations are creating a new problem for some villages. In Wad al Bilebli a local bird, *Um Awaidat*, builds its nests in the small branches of the *hashab* tree in June and July. Around

September, just when the crops ripen, they raid the farmers' fields to feed their chicks. The farmers fear that as the new *hashab* trees grow, they will harbour more and more of these birds which pose a threat to their food harvest.

Obstacles to sustainable forestry

One of the difficulties facing afforestation programmes is that environmental decline seems to feed on itself. The denuded areas prove the most difficult to regenerate, not least because the poorest people who are fighting for survival can seldom afford to wait for the slow process of afforestation. For most poor families, the first priority is food. Any attempt to halt the advance of the desert which does not start by enhancing their ability to meet their food requirements is unlikely to be sustainable.

Motivation

The main sources of livelihood in the project area are farming, animal breeding, seasonal wage labour and, to a lesser degree, gum arabic production. The main crops cultivated include sesame—a drought-resistant crop with a high market price—groundnuts (the second most popular cash crop), millet, sorghum, watermelon, cucumber and *karkadeh* (*Hisbiscus sabdritta*), used mainly for making a local soft drink.

Large numbers of people are forced to sell part of their millet harvest, their staple food, to buy sugar, tea and other basic household goods. Unable to retain enough seed grain for the next farming season, they must rely on traders from outside the village to finance a share-cropping arrangement—the *sheil* system—which leaves them with a very small portion of the harvest. This situation has influenced the feelings of local people towards the project, and explains why food aid is part of the scheme.

The World Food Programme's package of food aid, designed to assist rural peasants after the devastating effects of the 1982-84 drought, began at the same time as the FINNIDA-assisted forestry project. This helped reduce urban migration. In the Kosti area, about 300-350 farmers receive five deliveries a year of flour, sugar, tea and cooking oil. Most farmers say food aid is an important incentive for their involvement with the project. In the village of El Rimta, which has the largest concentration of farmers in the region, people are unanimous about its importance. The fact that *hashab* seedlings grown in plantations—often planted with food aid as an incentive—have been more successful than those grown around households, bears witness to this.

Ahmed, a farmer in the Tendelti area village of Wad al Bilebli, says food aid is necessary if *hashab* plantations are to continue. Other crop yields have declined so badly that farmers cannot afford to wait the five years for the income from gum arabic.

Balla Musa, extension officer for the Tendelti project area, says, "Food aid is not only an incentive but also a weapon." Farmers receiving aid who fail to protect their plantations are warned that their food aid will be stopped.

But food aid is less of an incentive in villages with higher crop yields and alternative sources of income. In Wad Sakkak village near Kosti, where there is no water shortage and there are adequate crop yields, trees are valued for their own sake rather than solely as soil improvers. *Hashab* plantations are not fenced, since the people are willing to protect them. And community woodlots of mesquite trees are planted on already fertile clay soils. Household and school plantations are flourishing as a result of education and literacy programmes explaining the benefits of tree planting.

Farmers here are more secure. If crop yields are poor, they prefer to sell off a few animals rather than migrate for seasonal work. Since agricultural land is not scarce there is no pressure to cut down *hashab* trees if gum arabic yields and prices prove too low. These farmers do not need food aid as an incentive—many have already witnessed the detrimental effects of loss of tree cover in neighbouring villages. Even more important, they feel reassured that involvement in the project's activities will not threaten their livelihoods.

There are inherent dangers in providing food aid or cash incentives. Desperate farmers may be persuaded to take part in afforestation projects simply out of expediency. Mohamed Shiluk of Dongolavia village in the Tendelti area was the first farmer to plant mesquite trees on his private land. His plantation was not fenced and he guarded the seedlings until they grew into mature trees. Shiluk recalls his experience: "I built a hut on the farm and brought my family from the village to live here to guard this plantation. My children were very serious about the matter; they did not even allow an official forest guard on his camel to enter the field."

He was one of 117 plantation guards who were paid S£250 (US$56) each a month as an incentive to guard the seedlings during the first two years of growth. When the trees no longer needed protecting, the wages stopped. Now Shiluk is demanding that he be allowed to cut down the trees and has threatened to go to court.

"I have no more land to cultivate my crops. I have no alternative occupation. I need money to support my family. What can I do without this monthly wage which the forest office decided to stop?" Shiluk asked. Extension workers advised him on how to thin the mesquite and prepare the land for agroforestry during the rainy season. The offcuts from thinning the trees would provide him with fuelwood which he could sell.

Shiluk agreed to take part in the programme to solve his acute food shortages. Coaxed into participation by financial incentives rather than because of any personal commitment to the project's objectives, he now believes there has been a breach of contract. While Shiluk's reaction may be unusual, it stems from the fact that his participation in the afforestation programme had more to do with immediate survival than a broad perception of the way environmental degradation is undermining his own capacity to feed his family. And in this he is not alone. Farmers interviewed in the village of Dabbat Hamra, Kosti area, complained that lack of resources means that the *sheil* system might be their only option, even though this share-cropping arrangement often leaves them poorer. "We want support in kind—for example, the provision of seeds by the government," was their message.

These examples illustrate some of the difficulties in generating and sustaining motivation in afforestation projects. Without the active involvement of local people, the continuing battle against desertification may be fatally weakened.

Who owns what?

Confusion over the ownership of trees and user rights has led to the overexploitation of forest resources. Farmers require a licence to clear any part of a forest owned by the government and need a permit to fell trees on private land. But in practice farmers who plant trees on their own land usually feel that they own the trees. So when forestry officials prosecute peasant farmers for cutting down trees, it reinforces the view that all forests belong to the government. Since the "owner" is far away in Khartoum, most peasant farmers believe they can use the forest as long as they do not get caught, and some may cut more than they need for household needs.

To solve such disputes, the White Nile province forest department has drawn up a legal contract, to be witnessed by local chiefs, which clarifies the relationship between the project and the farmer. This guarantees that plantations will be harvested by owners, under the supervision of project officials, and that the income will belong to owners. Tree ownership is usually sorted out before forestry officials agree with farmers about managing and using plantations.

New forest laws now allow for individual, village and town ownership of forests to encourage exploitation of forests in ways that are compatible with national interests.

To graze, or to grow trees?

In the White Nile area there are competing needs for grazing and forest land. Animals are raised by both settled people and nomads. Farmers resort to animal husbandry to complement crop production; when harvests fail, they usually sell some of their animals to buy food and other household items. Traditionally, no land is reserved solely for grazing, and although during the rains there is some customary obligation to restrict animals to particular patches, most of the time they roam at will.

This is why seedlings and trees have to be protected by fencing, as large herds of livestock around towns and big villages can threaten the establishment of plantations. The fences also protect against felling by nomads looking for wood to make temporary camps during their seasonal migrations.

Sayed Yasin Mohmood/Panos Pictures

The project covers an area where there are competing needs for forest and grazing land. While fodder remains in short supply, woodlots need to be protected against livestock.

Project officials in Tendelti believe that food aid and cash payments for guards are essential to keep the plantations properly protected. However, they recognise the need for a balance between the process of restocking forests and restocking animal wealth. Once there are significant numbers of mesquite woodlots, there will be enough readily available fodder for the livestock. But while forests provide the only grazing areas, a plan has to be developed to involve nomadic groups in ways of minimising damage to plantations.

Competing thirsts

In most of the villages in the Kosti-Tendelti area there is an acute shortage of water. Where villagers do not have enough for their daily needs, it is difficult for project staff to persuade them to begin nurseries and plantations. Fatma, of Shawak village in Tendelti, has no doubt in her mind: "It is nonsense to speak about trees while we are thirsty. How can we use water for seedlings when we ourselves and our animals need it most?"

Rainfall is usually between 350-400 mm per year, but can fall even lower during droughts such as those of the 1980s. In 1983 rainfall in the Tendelti area dropped to 84 mm, and to 96 mm in the Kosti area in 1984. The only other water source is the White Nile and wells replenished by rainfed underground water supplies.

The size and scope of the water source depends on the drainage network, the slope and depth of the clay soils, the size of the catchment area and type of bedrock. For example, Um Hager lies in the reach of Khor Abu Habil, a huge water course that is flooded each rainy season, enriching the soil with clay. Water also accumulates in the surface depressions, providing water all year round. For this reason, one of the nurseries was set up there.

Most villagers depend on wells for their domestic water. There are wells in nine villages in the Tendelti area and in 10 villages in the Kosti area. The Abu Habil seasonal river helps replenish the wells in villages along or near its route, but if the river does not flow, many wells dry up.

Another source is boreholes and most of the Tendelti villages depend on these for their water supply. One borehole normally serves 5-10 villages. The main problems are with maintenance and the saltiness of the water. When project staff visited the villages, nearly half of the boreholes were out of order.

Surface water, seasonal and limited, provides water for animal consumption for three to four months a year, during and after the rainy season. Surface water sources include natural depressions and pools called *rahads* and man-made water holes known as *haffirs*.

The search for water consumes time and energy and depletes already meagre incomes. A jerry can (18 litres) of water costs S£3 (67 US cents) in the Tendelti area. Yousif Hussein of Dabbat Baida

Water scarcity threatens people's involvement in the project, as one woman pointed out: "How can we use water for seedlings when we ourselves and our animals need it most?"

village near Kosti explains: "It is difficult to pay for water, so we restrict it to that needed for human consumption. Water for domestic use and for our animals is usually brought by donkey from faraway wells. Yet a thirsty donkey would not be fit for the hard job, and providing fodder and water for the beast is in itself quite expensive."

Project staff usually try to provide water for the afforestation programme by excavating a *haffir* or enlarging existing boreholes. These are used to irrigate the seedlings in the temporary nurseries established near the plantations. Extension workers advise households to use their domestic waste water to water the seedlings.

Villages with a permanent source of water, such as Wad Sakkak in Kosti and Karmal in Tendelti, have been more willing to participate in the afforestation programme.

Under the Sudan-Finland Development Programme, research is being conducted into ways of improving water supplies. If these are successful, people will not have to travel as far in search of water, leaving more time for productive activities. Animals, too, will not need to migrate to project plantations in search of *haffirs*.

Conclusion

This study has examined the extent to which the project is achieving its objectives—to create a system for expanding and strengthening White Nile forest resources that will be sustainable using local and national resources. True sustainability will require not only an increasing awareness among farmers about the process of environmental degradation, but also positive steps to ensure that they are able to rely on their own resources to combat desertification and provide fuelwood and fodder.

A thorny problem

The study has confirmed that mesquite plantations help to halt rapid encroachment by the desert. Yet mesquite is not without its problems since inadequate management of woodlots has restricted its role simply to anti-desertification. Proper management could generate income from marketable fuelwood, which would create greater enthusiasm for afforestation.

The need for an effective management plan for mesquite woodlots cannot be overemphasised. However, there appears to be some uncertainty about future plans. Taina Veltheim, Finnish forest management and extension specialist for the project, says there is an argument for allowing mesquite to grow unrestricted since holding back the process of desertification is top priority. Yet Tapio Niemi, the former acting coordinator of the Sudan-Finland Forestry Project, believes that thinning or pruning of mesquite is long overdue.

No management plan exists that addresses the problems of farmers. The thorns of mesquite inhibit any very productive use of land planted with the tree. A solution to this problem could prevent farmers felling trees on a large scale because they need land to cultivate food crops. While spare land is still available this is not an immediate danger. But with a population growth rate of about 2.9% a year for a population of 25.2 million, this is a potential problem which must be addressed.

Tapping sources of income

It is vital that farmers have a dependable source of income if they are to support the process of afforestation. If they can feed their families without depending too heavily on income from gum arabic they can better endure the five years before gum can be tapped and sold. This is what is required to restore the gum arabic belt.

Many households are anxious to derive cash income from their *hashab* plantations. But previous and current experience highlights the difficulties of promoting a cash crop that is also expected to help halt the process of desertification. The danger is that *hashab* plantations may be cut down once again to make way for other cash crops such as sesame if and when the market price for gum arabic continues its fall.

Long-term climatic change, manifested by recurrent drought, has pushed the gum arabic belt farther south. But it has also been eroded by the activities of the Gum Arabic Corporation. Like many marketing agencies in developing countries, it pays producers less than world market prices. This threatens the continued cultivation of *hashab* by forcing farmers to switch to more profitable crops. Moreover, in the badly drought-stricken areas of the country, farmers are increasingly cutting down the *hashab* trees to make charcoal which they sell, forced to meet short-term needs at the expense of long-term benefits.

Woodstoves

This is an important aspect of energy conservation and the only aspect of the project specifically targeted at women but, despite considerable efforts, the programme has made little progress. It is difficult to obtain the clay and water to build the woodstoves and so it will be a long time before they reduce the pressure on fuelwood.

Plantations

The project is developing an extensive system of mesquite and *hashab* plantations adapting the latest Finnish nursery technology. Field surveys show that appreciable areas have been planted, and these have halted the movement of sand dunes into the villages. For this, most villagers are grateful. Professor Abdel Nour, general manager of the FNC, is also happy with the project. He says: "It is one of our successful projects where something can be seen to be working." His view is shared by Sudanese and Finnish foresters working on the project. Their hope is that the restored forests will develop greater diversity as some natural species, benefiting from increased soil nutrients, may re-establish themselves.

Management
Although FNC officials express satisfaction with the project's progress and are committed to it, some problems need to be addressed. Taina Velthiem noticed that at Kosti the Sudanese say "this is a FINNIDA project" and "this is an Enso project." This seems to betray some unease about the way the scheme is managed. The management structure matches a Sudanese official to a Finnish worker at the two project offices in Tendelti and Kosti, but there is lingering resentment that the Finnish workers control the budget. Though Sudanese officials know all the budget details, they do not take decisions on its disbursement.

A question of sustainability
Significant progress has been made by the project but this study shows that the threat of environmental degradation remains, and that this threat is rooted in rural poverty.

It seems that the concept of integrated forestry has not been sufficiently thought through. The testimony of the rural people shows that the greatest danger to the project's success is the lack of provision for alternative sources of income. While this is certainly not a concern for foresters alone, no afforestation programme can be sustained if it does not take this into account.

The project is using advanced technology to produce impressive results. But this approach is the subject of debate. Are the high-tech, quick-results methods implemented by Enso appropriate for Sudanese conditions? Will the Sudanese government have the funds to continue these projects after Finnish aid ceases? There is a danger that these impressive results cannot be sustained. Or is there an argument for using such advanced technology because the environmental conditions are such that this is the only way to

Sayed Yasin Mohmood/Panos Pictures

Shifting dunes lap against the edge of the village of Dabbat Baida, covering farms and homes with layers of sand. Mesquite fencing is proving an effective barrier and soil stabiliser.

achieve any significant results?

Pekka Pesonen, an Enso official, maintains that the system is not high-tech, and that the most important question is whether or not it produces satisfactory results. He defended the use of Finnish technology, such as the plastic Enso pots: "We began using Enso pots because they had been proven to work well in Finland, and trials showed that they would work well in Sudan."

But the real test is whether Sudan can replicate the technology when using largely local resources. Taina Veltheim concedes that the present nursery system will collapse as soon as FINNIDA withdraws funding. Some FINNIDA officials also acknowledge that the White Nile Rural Forestry Development Project is not sustainable. Now they face a serious dilemma: should they hand over the project in 1993 as planned, in which case it is clear that without their financial support the work will grind to a halt; or should they continue to fund an otherwise unsustainable project? The issue is still being discussed. FINNIDA's predicament highlights the danger of implementing a high-tech, high-cost approach.

Most local people and foresters working with the project appear confident about their ability to continue, if Finnish funding is sustained. But when Nicholas Atampugre, editor and coordinator of the study teams, visited Tendelti nursery, he remarked how much it resembled a "mini Finland". At present, Finland provides everything from tractors, spare parts and nursery equipment to the coffee for workers. "If this stops," said one Tendelti official, "I don't know what we'll do."

Tapio Niemi of Enso, extension specialist and former acting coordinator of the Sudan-Finland Forestry Project, indicated that the problem of how the project would continue without Finnish aid had not been the agency's immediate concern. Within the Sudanese government, too, the problem of the project's future does not seem to have been properly addressed. Officials appear to have taken continuing Finnish financial assistance for granted.

The central nurseries at Kosti and Tendelti are due to be handed over to the government of Sudan in 1991 and 1992. Whether the Sudanese economy will be in a position to absorb the costs—especially of machinery used in seedling production, transportation and planting—is debatable. So, too, is whether a future government will consider it a priority.

Is there a cheaper way of slowing down what is undoubtedly severe environmental degradation? The evidence suggests that villagers hardest hit by environmental decline are understandably more concerned about their own survival than about trees. The gradualist approach, relying primarily on local resources, will take years to show positive results. Enso official Pesonen considers that the rate of desertification in the project area is so serious that an urgent solution has to be found. The gradualist approach alone cannot solve the problem.

The issue is not whether the villagers appreciate the importance of forest cover. The difficulties stem from the extent of rural poverty in the region. Because positive, visible results from afforestation take so long to materialise, it is difficult to generate and sustain motivation among poorer villagers.

The study also reveals that local people are not directly involved in decisionmaking. Although village committees work with extension officers, management decisions are taken by FINNIDA and Sudanese project staff. This may well result in effective short-term management, but there is always the danger that it will stultify local initiative, which is a vital component of sustainability.

This could prove to be a major stumbling block, and it highlights the importance of generating genuine local involvement. Many farmers echoed the opinion of Abdalla, the farmer from Um Damir village who felt constrained by all the advice from project staff. It had limited his sense of personal involvement with the project and discouraged him from trusting his own instincts about working with the trees on his land and thus from gaining practical experience. When questioned about mesquite thinning and agroforestry, he said: "We can do nothing but observe the directive of the officials and obey the orders of the government."

Select Bibliography

Documents of the Ministry of Foreign Affairs, Finland

"Sudan: Consulting Programme in Forestry and Forest Industries, Report of the Evaluation Mission", February 1982

"Sudan:Afforestation Programme, Report of the Evaluation Mission", March 1985

"Sudan: Forestry Sector Programme, Report of the Evaluation/ Appraisal Mission to the Sudan-Finland Afforestation Programme Phase IV (1986-88)"

"Sudan-Finland Forestry Programme, Phase V (1989-1993): White Nile Rural Forestry Development Project"

Hirovoner, S., "Factors affecting the attitude of villagers towards the afforestation programme—a socio-economic case study in the Tendelti/Kosti areas", FINNIDA Technical Report No 11, 1988

Hakulinen, M. and Luukkanen, O., "Socio-economic aspects of tree planting in the Tendelti area, Central Sudan—results of the drought years 1984/85", FINNIDA Technical Report No 10, 1987

Other Sources

Goda Hussein, S. E. D., "A preliminary study of soils under *Acacia senegal*", Sudan Silva 25, 1983

Baxter, "Women and Environment in the Sudan", paper presented at the workshop on Women and Environment, Khartoum, Sudan, 1981

"Environmental Review for the Western Agricultural Marketing Board, University of Khartoum", Institute of Environmental Studies, 1984

The East Usambara Catchment Forest Project, Tanzania

The first draft of this report was written by **Christopher Mwalubandu,** a journalist with the *Daily News*, Dar es Salaam. The work was completed by **Anthony Ngaiza**, coordinator of studies at the Tanzania School of Journalism. They were assisted by **Errics E M Kazungu** of the NGO Malihai Clubs of Tanzania who studied the environmental aspects; **Hadija Ramadhani** of the community forest section of the Ministry of Tourism, Natural Resources and Environment; **Pudenciana Temba,** a journalist with the *Daily News*, who examined women's involvement in the project; and **Bwire Musalika**, photographer.

Learning from the Past?

"Aren't FINNIDA the same people who sponsored Sikh Saw Mills and caused a lot of destruction in our area?" asked Hadija Idd Musa of Misalai village. "Sikh Saw Mills ended up almost turning the area into a semi-desert by logging trees haphazardly and destroying roads with their heavy-duty trucks, never repairing them," she explained. "Those guys valued money and nothing else," accused Idris Abubakar, 45, also of Misalai village. "Like ancient slave traders, they put money above everything else."

FINNIDA has a poor reputation in the East Usambaras because of its support for Sikh Saw Mills. The company became very unpopular in the 1980s for its "blind exploitation" of forests for industrial timber. Villagers in the Amani forest associate it with bad memories of land degradation, torn-up roads, soil erosion and muddied streams and water supplies.

The East Usambara Catchment Forest Project (EUCF) is an attempt by FINNIDA, and the local forestry authorities, to put this past behind them. Rather than timber exploitation, it is concentrating on watershed protection, conservation and sustainable use of the forests. After several years of planning and delays, work in the field began in March 1991. The project has a delicate task ahead—finding compromises between the many different users and uses of the forest.

The Usambaras

A black sky hangs heavily over the thick rainforest. Above the trees, as far as the eye can see, stretches the mountain range. It rises abruptly from the lowlands and is bounded by escarpments, producing a deeply dissected plateau often covered with drifting fog.

These are the East Usambara Mountains of northeastern Tanzania. About 40 km long and 10 km wide, they cover a rectangular area of some 40,000 hectares, taking in two districts,

Muheza and Korogwe, in Tanga region. They are part of a chain of isolated mountains called the Eastern Arc, which owe their origin to earth movements probably more than 25 million years ago.

These mountains have remained stable—geologically and climatically—for millions of years, and contain many plants, insects and animals unique to the region. For example, 14 species of lizards are unique to the area, seven types of chameleons and 35 types of millipedes. The forests also contain some of the rarest birds in Africa. They are also a vital water catchment area, feeding the Sigi River which is the main water source for nearby Tanga town and the surrounding region.

The East Usambaras have an ancient history. There is evidence of people living here in the early Iron Age. Ancestors of the Washambaa, the main tribe in the area today, ruled the mountains in the eighteenth century. Large-scale forest clearing started in the late nineteenth century, when Tanganyika (renamed Tanzania after uniting with Zanzibar in 1964) was a German colony. It was the Germans who first designated certain areas as forest reserves. They also founded an agricultural research station in Amani and set aside 300 hectares as a botanical garden, which still exists today. Attempts to establish coffee plantations, however, met with little success due to a combination of diseases and poor yields. After the First World War, Tanganyika became a British mandate and tea estates became the main large-scale commercial enterprise.

With independence in 1961, forest clearing for food and cash crops accelerated. Small-holder farmers invaded forests in search of more land, especially to grow cardamom and other spices. "The only thing we knew how to do was to clear the forests," recalls 79-year-old Athman Rashidi of Mikwinini village. He adds: "Unfortunately it has taken us decades to realise the folly of this—after the damage has been done."

"Wooden gold"

Commercial exploitation of the rich timber resources of the Usambaras began during the German colonial period, but developed on a grander scale in the 1960s. In recent years the main logger has been Sikh Saw Mills (SSM), first as a private company and then, after nationalisation in 1971, as a parastatal organisation—part of the Tanzania Wood Industries Corporation (TWICO).

Since 1977, Sikh Saw Mills has been supported in its activities by FINNIDA. As well as management advice, Finland has provided equipment such as chainsaws, bulldozers, skidders for moving logs, and gigantic Finnish-made "Sisu" logging trucks. A high-capacity peeler for making plywood has also been installed.

The felling of trees by Sikh Saw Mills caused havoc in the forest. Workers were selective in the trees they took, concentrating on the highest value species, particularly *Mtambara* (*Cephalophoera usambarensis*). In the felling process, many surrounding trees were damaged by falling branches and by the heavy logging and road construction equipment. Not only was the forest harmed, but public roads leading down the mountain were badly churned up by the heavy logging trucks, causing serious problems for other users.

Apart from Sikh Saw Mills, the Usambara forests were also invaded by individual pit-sawyers from other Tanzanian regions, especially Iringa and Mbeya. Even Kenyans, from Kisii district, flocked to the Usambaras in pursuit of the "wooden gold". Pit sawing involves the felling of individual trees, cross-cutting the trunks and rolling the logs onto frameworks, usually over pits. Planks are then sawn off by hand with a large vertical saw operated by two workers, one above and one below the logs. Although less destructive than the mechanical logging carried out by Sikh Saw Mills, as it does not involve the use of trucks or other heavy machinery, pit-sawing has added to the pressure on the forests.

The cardamom connection

Logging is not the whole story. Following on behind SSM and pit-sawyers, farmers have moved into many areas, exploiting the clearings left in the forest to plant cardamom (*Elettaria cardamomum*), a tall herb with large leaves. Since the early 1960s, cardamom cultivation has become big business in the area.

A member of the ginger family, cardamom grows well on freshly cleared forest soil. Its pods are used as a spice, especially in Asian food, as well as in some medicinal preparations, and fetch a high price in local markets. Cardamom takes four years before it starts producing, but in the Usambaras its cultivation is not sustainable.

After 10 years the soil is exhausted. Farmers then replace it with maize and other less demanding crops in order to eke out a few more harvests, before finally abandoning the land. Subsequent regeneration of the forest happens slowly, if at all, and any trees left standing on the cardamom plots then become vulnerable to high winds, and may be blown over—thus intensifying the rate of forest destruction.

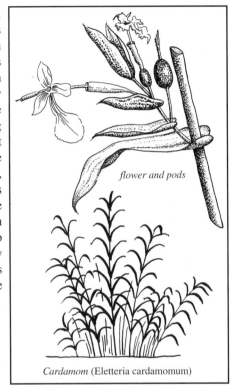

flower and pods

Cardamom (Eletteria cardamomum)

An international outcry

Regular visits by scientists studying the forest and its wildlife meant that the damage to the Usambara forests did not go unnoticed. Concerned individuals and organisations at both local and international level began joining forces in a bid to rescue the "Usambara Treasure".

In May 1985, an article in *New Scientist* magazine expressed concern about the disappearance of the African Violet *(Saintpaulia confusa)*—a small plant with delicate blue flowers, which had been identified as native only to the Usambaras. Its disappearance was blamed on the excessive logging activities. It did not take long before the spotlight was turned on FINNIDA.

Professor Olov Hedberg of Uppsala University, Sweden, wrote

to the director general of FINNIDA, Kai Helenius, in February 1986 expressing his concern. In September of that year, about 60 participants at an international conference on Tropical Entomology signed a resolution protesting against FINNIDA's support for logging activities. But the pressure did not stop there. Other eminent scientists also wrote to FINNIDA to put on record their disquiet about the damage being done with Finnish aid. Articles denouncing the logging appeared in the Tanzanian and Finnish press, with questions raised about why logging was taking place at all in such environmentally valuable forests.

FINNIDA's controversial role

It has never been FINNIDA's intention to damage the Usambara forests. Their assistance to Sikh Saw Mills started in response to a high-level request from the Tanzanian government, according to FINNIDA forestry advisor Tapani Oksanen. "On a visit to Finland, President Julius Nyerere specifically appealed to us to help develop the country's forest industries."

To provide a basis for this, an inventory survey was carried out in 1977 by the Finnish consulting company Jaakko Pöyry. Its terms of reference were to ascertain if there were sufficient timber resources to justify commercial logging. Accordingly, it recorded only commercially valuable tree species, and took no special note of the conservation or watershed value of the forests.

The survey concluded that there was plenty of timber available in the East Usambaras, and that an estimated 12,180 hectares would be suitable for logging. This provided the green light for Sikh Saw Mills to step up its logging in the area, but this time with highly efficient Finnish equipment.

The results of the survey soon became suspect as the "allowable" cut determined by the survey proved unrealistically high. A second inventory was therefore made in 1983. Conducted by the same consultants, this covered only a small portion of the best forest, and extrapolated from that. Its conclusions were very similar to the first survey, the main difference being that the figure for the area allegedly suitable for logging was revised downwards by 5%.

These inventories have since come in for heavy criticism, both at the technical level for the dubious assumptions they made, and because they completely ignored the conservation and other wider values of the forest.

Criticism has also been levelled at another Finnish consultancy company, EKONO, which was responsible for monitoring Sikh Saw Mill's operations in the Usambaras as part of its contract to provide management assistance to TWICO. According to Dr Jeff Sayer—the head of IUCN's Forest Conservation Programme, who visited the area in 1985—EKONO staff appeared to be unaware of the biological value of the forests in which they were operating and did not recognise the harm to the environment caused by their activities; or if they did, they did nothing about it.

Although FINNIDA officials were anxious to stop the growing international uproar, they were not prepared to accept full responsibility for the damage that had been done. The director general, Kai Helenius, argued that Finnish assistance was largely technical and aimed at replacing obsolete equipment as well as providing spare parts to keep the plywood mill in operation. Furthermore, since unemployment is a major problem in the region, it would not be advisable if the many people employed by Sikh Saw Mills were to lose their jobs. In any case, he argued, "it is estimated that 90% of the Usambara forest has been destroyed during the last 100 years. In this process, the impact of industrial logging activities does play a role, but a marginal one." He said the main threat came from land hunger and pit-sawyers.

Looking back, Finnish experts who were involved at the time admit that the logging did get out of control. According to Eero Reinius, of Jaakko Pöyry, too much emphasis was placed on meeting targets for logging output, irrespective of the environmental damage being caused, or even the economics of the process. He describes as "tragic" the way such superb timber was wasted by Sikh Saw Mills through bad logging practices and inefficient sawmills.

A definitive survey

In response to the increasingly vociferous criticism, and while logging was still going on, FINNIDA drew up plans in late 1985 for a third, and much more detailed, survey of the area. Named the

Amani Forestry Inventory and Management Plan Project (AFIMP), this was carried out by two other Finnish consulting firms, FINNMAP and Silvestria. It included an aerial survey of the forests, together with extensive fieldwork in which teams of botanists and foresters painstakingly crisscrossed the forest on foot, noting the exact species distribution both of trees and other plants. As well as detailed information on the state of the forest, its aim was to come up with a comprehensive management plan for the area, taking into account the conflicting needs of different users of the forest.

To ensure that the conservation angle was fully considered, the project was carried out in close coordination with the International Union for Conservation of Nature and Natural Resources (IUCN), now known as the World Conservation Union, which had already been working in the area for some time, and which until then had been a staunch critic of the uncontrolled logging. With Norwegian funding, IUCN conducted a series of complementary studies of the watershed properties of the area. IUCN was also asked to join the supervisory board of AFIMP, which included representatives from

David Dahmén Greenlink/Panos

The forest in the Usambara Mountains is a rich biological resource of international significance, but it also represents local livelihoods and national revenue. Whose priorities should take precedence?

all the Tanzanian and Finnish agencies involved.

The AFIMP inventory took more than a year to complete and produced a mass of useful data. Well before it was complete, it was clear that many of the concerns about logging in the area were valid. It provided ample evidence of the extensive damage being caused by mechanised logging, and showed that not only were the original assumptions of the earlier surveys suspect but that the management recommendations made at the time—such as to avoid steep slopes and areas near streams—were being largely ignored.

As a result of the AFIMP survey and the mounting international criticism, a decision was finally taken. At a meeting of the AFIMP management board in October 1986, Sikh Saw Mills agreed to stop logging in the mountain forests of the East Usambaras from the end of the year, and instead to switch their attention to forests in the lowlands and elsewhere.

But the damage had already been done. Areas opened up through the previous heavy logging, for example, were being rapidly colonised by *Maesopsis eminii,* an invasive tree that prevents regeneration of other plants, in particular a number of important indigenous tree species.

Better late than never?

The Tanzanian government is concerned about the deterioration of forest cover. "The energy crisis of the '70s has been translated into the wood crisis of the '80s and '90s," says Elifadhili Mnzava, director of forestry in the Ministry of Tourism, Natural Resources and Environment. "We have to act now or perish." If the forest disappears, so does the possibility of sustaining balanced land use which in turn provides goods and services for the local and wider community.

It is difficult to understand why the government has taken so long to translate this concern into action. Forested land outside special reserves has long been considered an inexhaustible resource, to be cleared for agriculture or cattle raising when desirable. The government has appeared indifferent to the uncontrolled exploitation of forests for fuelwood and industrial timber.

From a narrow economic point of view, the forestry sector's

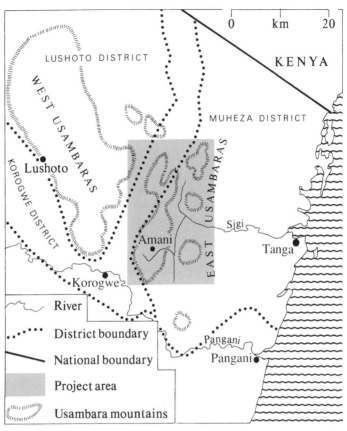

contribution to Tanzania's GDP has been marginal, and this has been reflected in the low priority it has received in the allocation of public resources. For example, the allocation of national funds for the catchment programme in the 1989/90 government budget was only US$20,500. At the same time, officials admit that the real value of the contribution of the forestry sector in terms of water catchment, climatic pollution buffering, and the provision of fuel, building materials and other produce, has been enormous.

The government says it recognises that current land use practices and the rapid growth of the rural population are contributing to deforestation. There seems to be growing awareness in government circles of the extent to which deforestation of catchment areas endangers water supplies and biological diversity. The Tanzania Forest Action Plan (TFAP), drawn up under the international Tropical Forestry Action Plan initiative, clearly aims at converting this heightened awareness into effective action, by designing projects which promote the development of water catchment management and the conservation of unique ecosystems such as the East Usambaras.

The government has been blamed for taking action too late, only after a major assault had been launched on the forests. The explanation given by the Ministry of Lands, Natural Resources and Tourism is that "the government could not come up with a solution overnight [and] a series of expert consultations had to be made." Government inaction, according to the former director-general of the National Environment Management Council, Godfrey Kamukala, "has affected the industrial and agricultural base for the entire Tanga region which depends on the continued and consistent water flow from the East Usambaras".

The East Usambara Catchment Forest Project

The East Usambara Catchment Forest Project (EUCF) is a response to the call for action to save the Usambaras, and is a follow-up from the AFIMP study and the management plan it produced. Its stated aim is to maintain "essential ecological processes and biological resources" for the people of the Tanga region as well as for the international community. It also aims to allow the utilisation of forest-related products by the local communities in a "rational and sustainable manner".

FINNIDA is providing a grant of US$32 million to underwrite the project, while the Tanzanian government has promised to contribute US$51,000, comprising salaries for the permanent and casual staff, and routine office expenses.

Management of FINNIDA's input to the project has been sub-contracted to the Finnish National Board of Forestry, which will have two full-time advisors working in Tanzania. On the Tanzanian side, the project team is being formed from the existing Tanga Region Catchment Forest office, which comes directly under the

---

The four main components of EUCF :

● Nature conservation: to establish and manage the Amani Nature Reserve in order to preserve the area's biological diversity. The aim is to develop forest areas known to still possess rare species and designate them for protection.

● Catchment forestry: to stabilise the flow of the Sigi River and assure good quality water yields to the villages and growing industrial community in Tanga municipality.

● Plantation forestry: to encourage plantation forestry in order to increase wood supplies. Unless the wood needs of the area are met, it may be impossible to prevent further cutting of the forests. Some attempts have already been made by companies like SSM to develop plantations to provide timber both for its sawmills and Tanga region in general. EUCF plans to complement such efforts.

● Institutional support: to improve the Forest Division's capacity to plan and manage natural forests for multiple purposes. This will include staff training, and provision of housing and vehicles.

Forestry and Beekeeping Division of the Ministry of Lands, Natural Resources and Tourism.

The project's headquarters will be in the town of Tanga, although this idea has been challenged by many local people who insist that management operations have to be based at the project site if they are to ensure efficiency. Project officials argue that locating the headquarters at Tanga "would facilitate access to all parts of the East Usambaras, and allow them to maintain close contact with the regional administration and other agencies working in the project area". In the view of Matti Määttä, the Finnish National Board of Forestry project coordinator, who also worked on the AFIMP project, the town remains the only realistic option for the headquarters because of the difficult terrain of the project area.

The project area

About 80% of the East Usambaras falls within the Amani division of Muheza district. The forest reserves with the greatest timber potential and highest biological diversity fall within this division and most of the population resides there. Amani has an area of 316 sq km, of which one-third is forested. "This is Africa's holy land,"

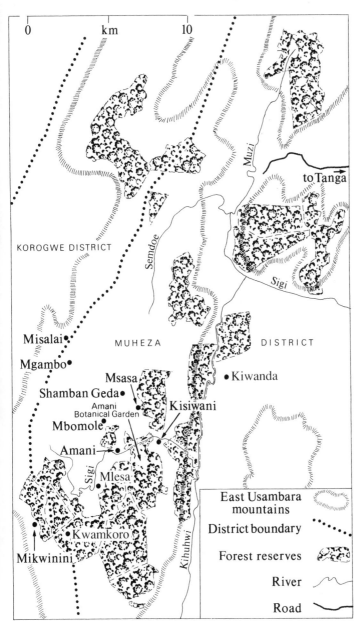

0   km   10

KOROGWE DISTRICT

Muzi

to Tanga

Semdoe

Sigi

Misalai

Mgambo

MUHEZA   DISTRICT

Msasa

Kiwanda

Shamban Geda

Amani
Botanical Garden   Kisiwani

Mbomole

Amani

Sigi

Mlesa

Kihuhwi

Kwamkoro

Mikwinini

East Usambara
mountains
District boundary
Forest reserves
River
Road

jokes the divisional secretary, Hamza Athmani.

Amani division has a population of 26,000 and is divided into two wards, Kisiwani and Misalai. Topograpy and land use patterns within the project area are complex. A patchwork of 16 forest reserves are separated by areas of public land, made up of tea plantations, small subsistence farms and some areas of public forest administered by the local community.

Based on the detailed results of the AFIMP survey, the idea is to divide the forest that remains into a number of zones. The best and most intact areas of forest will be designated nature reserves, and will be managed with biological conservation specifically in mind. Exploitation of resources will be strictly prohibited and the growth of *Maesopsis* will be actively discouraged.

Around these, a buffer zone will be created where controlled and sustainable exploitation can take place. There will also be areas, especially degraded patches of land on steep slopes, designated for watershed protection. *Maesopsis* will be maintained here until replaced by alternative vegetation. Public land, forest plantations and areas of cultivation will lie at the outer fringes of the protected areas. The aim is to preserve the integrity of the most valuable forests, while allowing sustainable uses within the buffer zone.

Theory into practice

These plans may look good on paper, but putting them into practice will be a different matter. Establishing the proposed zones will require the redesignation of the legal status of parts of the project area. For watershed protection reasons, some areas on steep slopes that are currently public land will be "gazetted" to make them official forest reserves. In such cases, farmers will be compensated for the land they lose. Other areas which are now forest reserves but have been heavily encroached by farmers may also be changed back to public land, in recognition of the fact that from a forestry point of view they are beyond salvation.

The project has yet to finalise plans for exactly which areas will be affected, or how these changes will be implemented—in particular, how farmers will be compensated for any loss of land or income. Although the intention is to avoid confrontation wherever possible and to minimise the effect on farmers' incomes, FINNIDA officials recognise that this may not always be easy.

How to deal with cardamom cultivation is a particularly difficult question. Within forest reserves, cardamom growing and other forms of encroachment are illegal, and the government in theory has the right to expel those responsible. According to the project document a lenient approach will be taken, and farmers will be allowed to continue harvesting their plots while the crop is still producing—but they will be banned from extending them. How these guidelines will be interpreted in practice is not yet clear. According to FINNIDA forestry advisor Tapani Oksanen, the Forest Division has already cut down cardamom plots in some areas, after nobody admitted owning them.

The project thus has a major task ahead of it in working out the necessary compromises with local people. Matti Määttä, the project coordinator, suggests that the easy areas should be approached first to build up the required experience for tackling the most controversial questions. In his opinion, it will be very important to be "sensitive" when it comes to implementing the project. For example, redefining forest reserves should be done to avoid existing *shambas* (farms) wherever possible.

Establishing nature reserves

A key objective of the project, in light of the international uproar created by conservationists, is the preservation of the rich biological diversity of the area. According to forest expert Patrick Akitanda, there are no other forests earmarked and managed for biological value in Tanzania today. "The main task is to design and create the Amani Nature Reserve", he says, "but it may be necessary to create nature reserves in other areas." He points out that any plans must take into account the importance of ensuring that the reserves, with their rich resource base, do not become isolated from the rest of the forest. There should be some continuity between the different areas so that the varied flora and fauna can flow freely between and flourish within the various zones.

Creating a nature reserve will involve specifying certain areas to be designated for protection and establishing adequate legal safeguards which can be enforced in the field. Whatever measures are taken will have to comply with current Tanzanian legislation. A short-term consultancy will advise on the legal implications. This phase, says Akitanda, should include public announcement of the plans so that compensation claims for loss of land and income can be assessed.

Boundaries of natures reserves will also have to be surveyed and marked out in the field, and corresponding maps produced. Boundaries of existing reserves are marked with rows of planted trees, and this has reportedly been a good means of preventing

fruit containing seed

Maesopsis eminii

encroachment. If a similar system is to be used for the Amani Nature Reserve, forest experts point out that the planting must be done with species which do not regenerate naturally, otherwise boundaries could rapidly become blurred.

Experts urge that a basic data bank be created to monitor the success of conservation activities. Remarkable amounts of data already exist; all that is required is to bring them together. Additional data on species not yet surveyed need to be collected, and this will require assistance from experts in Tanzania and abroad.

There will be an emphasis on the use of local expertise wherever possible. Plant specimens will be housed in the Lushoto herbarium, while reports will be gathered and collated in the Amani library and copied to the library of the Silvicultural Research Station in Lushoto. One of the directives of the Finnish coordinators of the project is that all research must contribute to the data bank.

Conservation is a major focus of the project. "But", warns Tapani Oksanen of FINNIDA headquarters, "not all the conflicting interests can be completely harmonised." He points out that conservationists will not be entirely happy because the project does not meet all their demands. "One conservationist on the appraisal team was in favour of ring-barking all *Maesopsis* trees [to kill them slowly] and kicking out all the farmers." He also doubts how realistic the calls are from some conservationists who argue that 600-metre-wide "bridges" of undisturbed forest are needed to connect the best pieces of intact forest to ensure that species can move from one reserve to another. This, he says, will be very difficult to achieve.

Collaboration with IUCN

The EUCF project was never intended to operate in isolation. From the outset it was seen as a partner to another project operating in Amani division, which was coordinated by IUCN.

The East Usambara Agricultural Development and Conservation (EUADEC) project, usually referred to as the IUCN project, was launched in 1988 as part of efforts being made by conservationists to halt deforestation in the area and to support sustainable forest management. IUCN was funded by the European Commission to implement the project for an initial period of three years, but it now seems likely that, provided current funding problems are sorted out, a much longer programme of activities will evolve. This may also cover villages in two neighbouring divisions, according to IUCN project manager Joseph Lindi.

The project's aim is to assist villagers in developing their own solutions to the problems of forest encroachment and diminishing forest resources. Its most important partners are therefore the local farmers.

"Philosopher kings"

Throughout the IUCN project, staff and local technical officers have worked with villagers, identifying their problems and potential solutions. Many options were considered and as a result new crops have been introduced, trees planted and agroforestry techniques tested. "We started on a small scale, but the aim was to build upon success by providing further assistance and by facilitating the spread of ideas and information between all the villages in the district," says Julius Ningu, an agronomist attached to the project. The project has also provided assistance for the expansion of Forest Division activities in the area, including the establishment of nurseries and demarcation of reserve boundaries.

The project has appointed one coordinator in each of the 13 villages covered. The conditions were that they had to come from the division itself and possess at least Ordinary-level secondary school education. They were then trained in communication and other skills related to environmental protection. Village coordinators are happy at the way the project has been received locally. Peter Kabimba, coordinator of Misalai, sums it up thus: "What has inspired the local people is that they have been involved in actually implementing the project. Things would not have got moving if they had been made to play second fiddle."

Forestry official Joseph Lindi, seconded to Amani by the Ministry of Agriculture and Livestock Development in 1987, bears considerable personal responsibility for the project's good reception. The reason for his success is clear. "All I did was to go from village to village, convening meetings at which the principal speakers were the villagers themselves. They related their problems

Cardamom growing near Msasa village. For many local people the spice is their sole source of cash income but it is productive only in the short term, leaving behind bare patches of exhausted soil.

and suggested solutions. This dialogue gave us credibility and the project was received with open arms," he explained.

As divisional secretary Hamza Athmani explained, "This man succeeded because he came to my people as someone needing to learn from them. The problem with many others who had come before him is that they came to us as philosopher kings."

The project was welcomed by the local population because it acts upon a variety of village problems and not merely environmental ones, according to Athmani. He adds a cautionary note, however, explaining that "the people are wary" about certain delicate issues such as the future of cardamom cultivation in the forests and pit-sawing. Both activities are highly lucrative and will not be given up readily. This is the heart of the dilemma. How does one strike the right balance between meeting the needs of the local community while at the same time carrying out necessary but unpopular measures?

Partners or rivals?

While the IUCN project deals with the local community as a target group and EUCF concentrates on catchment forest, the two projects share similar development objectives and cover the same area. The government believes that the coordination of their efforts would be beneficial. Indeed, the minister of state in the prime minister's office, Edward Lowassa, stressed that the government sees "these projects as one and the same. They must be coordinated to avoid duplication". At the beginning of 1991, both projects appeared to be facing some difficulties, although of different types. The IUCN project seemed threatened by funding problems, while the EUCF, though guaranteed of funding, was only just getting off the ground.

A forestry expert in the Ministry of Tourism, Natural Resources and Environment, Saidi Mbwana, who was part of the team that prepared the EUCF project document, thinks friction between the projects will be inevitable if they do not work together: "Coordination of these projects must be the bottom-line, if conflict and higher operational costs are to be avoided."

The question of how exactly to implement this coordination caused something of a rude awakening among the financing agencies and governments concerned. A meeting to clarify the situation was held in September 1990 in Switzerland, attended by officials from IUCN and the Finnish National Board of Forestry.

One area of cooperation suggested was the sharing of running costs by joint purchase of equipment. However, a major impediment is that existing FINNIDA procedure requires that all equipment be purchased through the Finnish government purchasing centre. Another idea being mooted within FINNIDA is that IUCN might be contracted to implement the nature conservation component of EUCF. Similarly, it may be appropriate for the EUCF project to take over some of the activities in the IUCN project, for example, those undertaken in cooperation with the Forest Division. At the minimum, both parties recognise the need for regular consultation between senior staff, and the exchange of information as well as documents and working reports.

It is undoubtedly encouraging to see serious attempts being made to streamline working relations between the two organisations. However, officials in the Ministry of Tourism, Natural Resources and Environment admit they are puzzled by the fact that the resolutions adopted at the meeting in Switzerland seem not to have been passed on, ostensibly because the meeting had no official status. Many who were interviewed for this study declined to be identified but expressed anger and frustration over the issue. "Whatever the reasons," complained a Tanzanian government official, "there is no justification for the financiers [FINNIDA] to keep us in the dark."

While the relationship with IUCN may well prove to be a productive one, the need to clarify it has been one of several factors which have delayed the implementation of the EUCF project.

Lost momentum

The EUCF project has had a long gestation. Although the AFIMP management plan was finalised in 1988, it is only now—more than two and a half years later—that the project is getting under way.

The causes for the delay are not entirely clear. FINNIDA officials in Dar es Salaam were tight-lipped when asked to comment. Financial limitations on the part of the Tanzanian government and continuing discussions between FINNIDA and IUCN have all contributed to the slow progress. Although eventually scheduled to start in September 1990, project officials were only appointed in February 1991. Finnish staff started work in the field in March.

Dr Robert Bensted-Smith, who worked for IUCN developing the plans for the EUADEC project, is highly critical of the delay. According to him, the project plans were discussed fully in April 1988 at a meeting in Tanga attended by all the relevant local officials and political leaders. "The Tanga people were ready to go ahead, and FINNIDA publicly stated their willingness to fund the programme if IUCN and the Forestry Division came up with a suitable proposal." The project could have started in early 1989, he believes, if IUCN, FINNIDA and the local authorities had "got their act together".

The delays have meant that "the whole momentum of the project has been lost", according to Dr Bensted-Smith, with the focus of the preparatory work shifting from Tanga to IUCN and FINNIDA headquarters in Nairobi and Europe. The initial local political support and enthusiasm, he says, have been replaced by the usual scepticism and weary acceptance of delays. With current project preparation procedures, how far is it possible to achieve real local participation and confidence in project planning? "The system of a succession of very hurried missions separated by time lags of unpredictable duration cannot work. Villagers need continuity. They need opportunities to chew things over amongst themselves and to ask questions. Their confidence should not be undermined by project personnel disappearing and all activity stopping until suddenly they reappear—and another flurry of activity takes place," he argues.

Back in Helsinki, Finnish officials deny that the preparatory period in this case has been unusually long, especially since the intention was to ensure a proper organisational framework. According to both Matti Määttä, the EUCF project coordinator, and Tapani Oksanen of FINNIDA, two and half years is "quite normal". They concede, however, that these kinds of delays do not help to encourage local participation in the planning of projects but say that "this is how the project cycle works".

Having finally sorted out the bureaucracy, Finnish officials are anxious to get started. The key question now is: What will the project bring to the Usambaras and their people?

Towards sustainable forestry

Given the controversy which surrounded Finnish assistance to Sikh Saw Mills, it has been imperative for the designers of the EUCF project to exercise maximum caution over the type of activities the project involves. The fact that the water catchment properties of the Usambaras, rather than their forestry potential, is the main focus of the project reflects this.

The project is starting at a time when public awareness of the importance of forests is gaining momentum. "The value of forests is obvious," says Bakari Kahela, 65, a member of Shamban Geda village council who is responsible for protecting the forest around the village from encroachment. He and his wife left Lushoto district in West Usambara for East Usambara in search of better farmland. "We left because that district is a sad example of indiscriminate tree felling and land degradation," says Kahela. They now understand better the effects of deforestation, he says, as they have seen the weather change over the past 40 years: "No dry season existed in the Usambaras until the senseless plunder of forests started in the '60s." Although there is no scientific evidence of a link between deforestation and decreased rainfall, the belief that one exists is widely held among local farmers.

EUCF project coordinator Matti Määttä is optimistic about its prospects. "There is a lot of expectation and commitment from both sides," he points out, "and I really hope it will be a success." In his view, success will depend on the extent of local people's participation and on whether the project is implemented in such a way that they do not feel it will destroy their livelihoods.

Local participation

The EUCF project document highlights the need for the project to benefit local communities directly. It provides no clear outline, however, of the practical nature of the relationship between local people and the project. Although some employment opportunities will be created, there appears to be no involvement of local people in management. The only indication so far of their involvement is a mention in the project document of plans to "inform" them about the project in June 1991, months after its scheduled beginning.

The villagers who were interviewed were unaware of the EUCF project. Most of them said they had only heard about it from the Panos evaluation team, and they wondered how it would be implemented. Women in the villages of Misalai, Mbomole and Msasa, for example, said they knew nothing about EUCF when the team interviewed them in August 1990, less than one month before the project was scheduled to start. Hadija Idd Musa, chairperson of Misalai, said it was the first time she had heard about it. Veronica Nkupe of the same village was not exactly surprised "to learn there is to be a FINNIDA project going on in my village, because they normally only involve us when implementation starts".

EUCF project planners are being blamed for "putting the cart before the horse". While they are aware that the cooperation of the local population is vital to the success of the project, they failed to involve them actively throughout the preparatory stages. Many villagers are well aware of the irony of contingency plans being made now to mobilise their support for the project and to convince them of the benefits of water catchment management. As one villager pointedly asked: "Will they abandon the project if we think that it is against our interests?" Meanwhile, FINNIDA and the Forest Department are preparing posters and planning seminars to disseminate the findings and requirements of the project.

Hungry for land

The problem of access to cultivable land is crucial in the area. "Most of the quarrels and complaints we receive from the villagers are related to land. There are more than 640 adults in this village and they all depend on land for food," pointed out Pius Pembea, Msasa village secretary.

Many years ago, East Usambara was regarded as a land of plenty. During the pre-colonial period, farming systems were small scale and in balance with the environment. On the whole, agriculture was practised in such a way so as not to endanger the long-term viability of the community. However, the development of tea estates and commercial logging and an increased population have decreased the amount of land available per family unit. "What is left is too small for the rest of us," complains Habib Musa, of

Petri Heinonen/Panos Pictures

As villages expand, the resulting deforestation is clear to see—yet access to cultivable land is crucial to the villagers' survival.

Kisiwani village. "Our grandchildren will be living with their backs to the wall."

Since they had not participated in the planning of the project, villagers were unsure how it would affect them. Those interviewed in the five villages likely to be affected by the creation of forest reserves were particularly apprehensive. Most of them said that any action to move them off their land would seriously affect their ability to survive. Unless villagers are given alternative means of meeting their basic needs, or can participate in the protection of the forests, encroachment will persist. Msasa village secretary Pius Pembea believes that any reduction in their land would force some people to leave the village. He warned: "The problem is complicated. I think the project is only looking at the issues at surface level." He felt that the traditional norms of society would be affected, adding that villagers are reluctant to give up their traditional lands. Reported government plans to resettle affected families in other villages such as Pangani, Handani and Korogwe were viewed with concern. These areas are not particularly fertile and the problem of food insecurity—which lies at the heart of forest encroachment—will undoubtedly arise.

FINNIDA officials deny that any such drastic moves are planned, stating that proposed boundaries for forest reserves have been deliberately drawn to avoid existing farming areas. The only exception is one area on steeply sloping land directly adjacent to Amani Nature Reserve. But in the absence of clear information at the village level, suspicions remain.

A prosperous young farmer in Shamban Geda village, Maulid Kipanda, says that if his farm had to give way to the forest reserves he would resist—because without the farm, he could not support his family of six. "I believe strongly in the preservation of forests—but taking away part of my farm is something else. You see, it would disrupt our family existence. It would put me in an extremely awkward position."

Because of the sensitivity of the issue, FINNIDA has been advised to take great care before proceeding further. IUCN project manager Joseph Lindi warns that the EUCF project could encounter problems in "conflict areas" near forest reserves, where villagers would be unwilling to part with their land for the sake of increasing reserve areas. "Force might have to be used to remove the smallholder farmers near reserves," Lindi says, "but this would be resented and so would be a bad start for the project."

Meeting basic needs

One of the cornerstones of sustainable forestry is its ability to ensure that people who live in the surrounding area meet their basic needs without damaging the forests. However, the dilemma is that it is those who are most dependent on forest resources who are least able to endure the slow process of afforestation. Yet it is they who must benefit directly from projects like EUCF, if the projects are to have any chance of success.

Like many other villagers, 65-year-old Bakari Kahela gets some extra benefit from the forest around the village. He has had a cardamom farm for the past 20 years. He also has 500 coffee plants inside the forest. The village government has now banned any extension of farms, and villagers are only allowed to continue harvesting from their existing plots. The purpose is to leave the forest around the village intact for some years to enable it to recover. Then people can again be allowed to exploit it in a controlled, "reasonable" way. This method of control has been successful mainly because local villagers are allowed to harvest from their existing cardamom farms, and therefore still earn some income.

According to official accounts, the villagers were advised by the IUCN project's village coordinator, Modi Nyimbire, who succeeded in getting the villagers' support. "We are glad they saw reason. Those farms will now be phased out naturally, because the increasing tree canopy will block sunlight penetration to the crops. We expect that regeneration on the forest floor will eventually overpower crops," Nyimbire said. "The villagers will finally have to stop and they know this." The hope is to promote cloves, coffee and tea farming as alternatives to cardamom cultivation, although they are unlikely to provide the same level of income.

But not all villagers are happy about the prospect of having their crops "phased out for the sake of the forest". Sylvester Mbiu, a retired tea estate worker at Misalai village, has about six acres of cardamom in the village forest from which he harvests 180 to 300 kg every year. "It would be unthinkable for me to stop maintaining my farm. No-one can convince me that cardamom harms the forest. No! That's a conspiracy." He warns: "If we are not given alternative means of meeting our basic needs, we will continue to rely on the forest for our survival even if it appears to be destroying the forest. After all, for whom are they protecting the forests?"

There are others who share this view and who would go to great lengths to ensure that their traditional farms are maintained. "We are faced with a difficult issue, because some villagers think we are about to threaten their very livelihood," says Saidani Hussein, a member of the Mbomole village council.

Who should manage the forests?

Forestry Division officials do seem to have realised that the retention of forest cover depends on the local people. Yet in practice many projects dealing with forest reserves still reflect colonial policies and legislation which emphasised forest protection and revenue collection. Professional foresters still perform the role of "protectors" of reserves and collectors of fees. To some extent, the EUCF project plans to adopt the same strategy, in spite of its questionable effectiveness. Six forest guards are to be employed at each field station in villages close to the forest reserves. Their main job effectively entails performing police duties.

This approach is questioned by Pius Pembea, who suggests that the responsibility of forest protection should rest with the village governments themselves "because they are in constant touch with ordinary people". Project guards, he says, are virtually powerless in this respect. "People will react by felling more trees. The presence of forest guards will mean little," he warns. "Rural development must be by the people rather than for the people."

Miraji Shekoloa, Mikwinini village secretary, believes the project will be beneficial, and is optimistic that villagers will respond positively, especially to the establishment of buffer forests and the development of individual woodlots. Nevertheless, he, too, was quick to point out: "We would prefer to manage buffer forests ourselves. We think a security system developed by the local community is more effective than one imposed from outside."

Conservationist Dr Bensted-Smith, however, questions how

realistic this is. He agrees that in certain areas, village management of the forests may be a good idea. "But not", he argues, "in forests where catchment protection and genetic resource conservation are critical." He sees a continued role for forest guards in such cases.

Commercial exploitation

After the experience of the Sikh Saw Mills operation, it is debatable whether any commercial exploitation at all should be encouraged. Conservationists, worried about the rapid loss of indigenous species, view any such proposals with suspicion. Yet the local people see the forests and the natural environment as existing to provide for their needs. For the government of Tanzania, any investment which promotes sustainable utilisation of the Usambaras is worthwhile, considering the marginal contribution of the forestry sector to the national economy at present. And the Forest Division contends that, if control over illegal exploitation is achieved, then some small-scale, manual commercial harvesting could be allowed.

The difficulty is that a real threat to sustainable commercial

Bwire Musaika/Panos Pictures

Some conservationists argue against any commercial exploitation of the forest. Others say controlled logging need not cause destruction and will provide much-needed revenue.

exploitation could develop if the area is seen to have the potential to generate significant income for private interests. Without effective local control of forest resources, private individuals interested in quick profits could move in and subvert the planned sustainable exploitation of forests.

Women's involvement

Women are often given too little opportunity to participate in development projects, even those with a declared intention of meeting the needs of rural people. So far, this project seems to be no exception. Women interviewed in the villages of Misalai, Mbomole, Msasa, Shamban Geda, Mlesa and Mgambo stated that they had not been involved in the planning process. When asked if they were willing to accept the EUCF project, most of them replied positively, because the project would assist them considerably if it achieves its declared goals. But like all villagers, they are concerned about the possible impact on household land holdings. They categorically oppose any reduction of their plots. Because of the geography of the East Usambaras, cultivable land is scarce and the people jealously guard the little land they possess. "Ask anyone here and you will find that most of the disputes we deal with from villagers are related to land holdings," says the Mgambo village secretary, Zaina Mwasoni.

In Africa, women are the direct users of forest products. This reflects traditional customs and norms which restrict men to certain kinds of jobs, and leave women with a multitude of household chores in addition to bringing up the children. It is women who normally fetch water, collect fuelwood, prepare meals and oversee the family's general welfare. Researchers have calculated that a rural Tanzanian woman spends about 16 hours a day performing duties related to the upkeep of the family. Often half of that time is spent searching for fuelwood and fetching water. Women in the East Usambaras are no exception, although they are luckier than some, since water and fuelwood are comparatively plentiful in the area.

Most women say they are aware of the need to protect the environment in the East Usambaras, surrounded as they are by forests. However, environmental protection becomes contentious as soon as it means they have to stop activities which generate much-needed income. As Neema Chavala of Msasa village explained: "We entirely depend on cash from the sale of spices which we grow in the forests." Most of the women argued that acceptable methods of agriculture could still be applied in the forests without disturbing the environment in the way researchers and biologists fear.

The consensus among women was that they would only stop activities in the forest if the project would provide alternative income-generating jobs. "If the project will employ us and pay enough money for us to buy sugar, meat, clothes, shoes and other things, we are prepared to surrender our land," stated Nasemba Karo, of Mlesa village. The women point out that forest conservation practice is already changing because the village government, under instructions from the district authorities, is already preventing them from cultivating farms deep in the forest.

A popular employer

The Commonwealth Development Corporation (CDC) is very popular among women because it does offer them employment. It pays them reasonably well for part-time tree planting work and it also employs many women in the nearby tea estates weeding, picking tea, supervising and performing other duties in the processing factory. "If it were not for the Corporation," commented 45-year-old Catherine Achi, of Mgambo village, "our lives would have been very difficult." The tea estates also employ children, for which many families are grateful. "This relieves us parents, as the children get money to buy their own uniforms and pay school tuition and food fees," explained Achi.

Because women are rarely included in the planning process, their priorities are overlooked by most projects. In this case, if they had been consulted it would have become clear that they had a definite preference for planting medicinal trees and herbs. Amani is known throughout Tanzania as a source of medicinal herbs. A recent study by Tanzanian botanist C K Ruffo, carried out in collaboration with IUCN, established that as many as 185 medicinal plants are found in the East Usambaras and that they have been used to treat 65 different diseases or ailments.

The lack of health services in most villages underlines the importance of medicinal plants. Women and children have to walk long distances through mountainous terrain to reach the limited medical facilities available, usually those at the Amani Malaria Research Institute. Health centres in tea estates are restricted to employees. Habiba Shomari of Mlesa village says, "If it were not for the medicines we get from forests, many of our children would have died before the age of one." This view was echoed by Sophia Kipungu of Shamban Geda village: "I only take my children to hospital or the dispensary when I have had no success with all the herbs I know that cure a particular ailment." Like many others, she has more confidence in herbal medicines than in modern medicine. The most common ailments treated with herbs are flu, malaria, headaches, and muscle, chest, stomach and back pains, as well as certain gynaecological problems.

Women would also like to grow fodder for dairy cattle. A non-governmental organisation operating in the area distributes cows to villagers on the condition that all calves produced will be given to other villagers. The arrangement is working so cheaply and smoothly that many women can now afford to buy more cows.

As well as needing fuelwood, women would like shade-giving trees near their houses. They are also interested in fruit trees, such as avocado and mango. "It would be good if the fruit trees are developed as part of the project because my children, and indeed the entire family, would benefit from them," remarked Aisha Akyoo of Msasa village. The women were less enthusiastic about the prospect for timber trees because, according to them, their husbands pocket all the money from such sales.

Conservation for whom?

No other issue has provoked more controversy in the East Usambaras than the conservation of genetic resources. Although the principle of managing natural resources in a way that will maintain their long-term value makes sense, it is debatable whether a country like Tanzania, one of the least developed in the world, should in practice carry this out when many local children are malnourished or suffering from lack of medical care. How do you manage resources for the benefit of future as well as present generations and at the same time meet the day-to-day needs of the surrounding communities?

In other words, it is all very well to talk about the wonders of Mother Nature and the amazing array of undocumented species in the Usambaras, but what does this mean to an ordinary farmer desperately trying to eke out a living and, from necessity, encroaching on the forest? "You cannot think about 'conserving genetic resources' when you have an empty stomach," says Saleh Omari, 71, a village elder.

Questions are being raised at the national level about whether genetic conservation is a luxury the country cannot afford. "Allocating resources for a project like this is tantamount to allocating foreign reserves for space exploration research," said one member of parliament, Charles Kagonji, who comes from the Usambaras.

The Finnish government says it is committed to the project "for the betterment of Tanzanians and mankind", but explains that it can only supplement Tanzanians' own efforts towards the conservation of their natural heritage. Says the Finnish ambassador to Tanzania, Kari Karanko: "What Finland can contribute to the exercise is minimal. The biggest share of the burden will have to be shouldered by Tanzanians themselves." The ambassador stops short of saying that Tanzania is not fulfilling its share of the exercise but he did state that, "No white man can conserve that forest for you. Only the black man can do that. Our efforts are merely supplementary." This is a viewpoint shared by project coordinator Matti Määttä: "Tanzania could have done a lot in the area of nature conservation and should not have waited for us to do the job." He adds, however, that the Tanzanian authorities have lately been cooperating well with the relevant Finnish organisations.

These are complex questions and the answers have so far eluded planners and politicians alike. Local people do not appear to recognise the need for preserving species, or to appreciate the value of biological diversity. Few are aware, for example, of how rare and unusual are the flora and fauna in the mountains. Villagers in Shamban Geda said that most of the plants with medicinal value were small herbs which did not need special protection.

Given this, perhaps natural, scepticism, the question of whether villagers should be expected to bear the costs of conservation is a pertinent one. If conservation is seen as a priority, the substantial costs involved may have to be borne outside the village, and indeed outside the country. After all, preserving biodiversity is to the benefit of the international community, not just Tanzania. But this will require the long-term commitment of conservationists worldwide.

Space invader

The invasion of forest by the tree *Maesopsis eminii* poses special problems for conservationists. Known as *Muzizi* in Swahili, this tall thin deciduous tree abounds in Uganda and Zaire and occurs also in Zambia, Kenya and Angola, as well as Ghana and Liberia in West Africa. In Twi, a language spoken among the forest dwellers of the Ashanti region in Ghana, it is called *Nyamedua* (God's tree) and has special religious significance, being used for carving stools associated with royal ceremonies.

Introduced into the Usambaras in 1913, *Maesopsis* has successfully colonised many of the areas opened up by logging activities, and is preventing the regeneration of other species. This opportunistic tree produces numerous seeds, which are dispersed over a wide zone by the hornbill, a common bird in the mountains. Scientists say its survival and growth rates are so high that within three years most saplings are mature enough to produce more seeds. As a result, several areas in the East Usambaras are now dominated by *Maesopsis*.

Researchers are worried that the tree may in the long run degrade catchment quality, because wherever it grows there is little or no regeneration of primary forest trees. *Maesopsis* produces only a thin leaf litter, which does little to prevent surface run-off during the rains. Most of the species which it is displacing, however, produce thicker ground litter and are thus better at soaking up rain water and releasing it slowly over subsequent weeks.

"This species dominates other trees and the only way to stop it is by eliminating the species itself," says Joseph Lindi, IUCN project manager. Conservationists argue that it should never be planted in the area.

Bwire Musalika/Panos Pictures

The uncontrolled logging of the past, in part supported by FINNIDA, left large clearings which have been taken over by the fast-growing maesopsis tree at the expense of other, more productive species.

But many local people interviewed held a different view. Many did not think *Maesopsis* posed any threat to their day-to-day needs, and most of them said they were glad to see such massive growth of the tree in the areas left bare by Sikh Saw Mills. According to them, the species has created a good micro-climate, which has benefited their cash crops, particularly cardamom. But they commented on its limited value as fuelwood, because "it burns like paper" and is too light to make good charcoal.

The problem of *Maesopsis* raises the familiar problem of conflict of interests. Conservationists are justifiably alarmed about the rapid expansion of *Maesopsis* and the threat that it poses. The local people, however, are too happy to have tree cover to worry about its limited value. The challenge facing the project team is to find ways of using *Maesopsis* productively and then to popularise its use in the community, so that villagers' sources of income can be diversified. This seems to be the most practical way of tackling the problem.

According to conservationist Dr Bensted-Smith, "it should not be difficult to start controlling *Maesopsis*". He argues that if local people were encouraged to cut and use the tree, by waiving any royalties on it, "they would be eager to exploit it". He points out that the tree is used widely for general purposes in other parts of Africa, and tests by a forester in Amani found that it was suitable for making furniture. But while other, higher-grade timber is still available locally, it may be difficult to encourage its commercialisation.

Conclusion

A question that critics will be asking is whether FINNIDA really has changed its tune and committed itself to conserving the environment, rather than focusing on purely commercial forestry considerations. The project document certainly suggests so and demonstrates a clear intention to promote environmentally sound and sustainable forestry. But can the project turn these ambitious plans into reality, given the social complexities involved and the many conflicting interests? With work only just starting, it is too early to draw any firm conclusions.

The success of the project is going to hinge on establishing effective community participation. Yet most of the villagers interviewed were unaware of the impending project. Participation at the planning stage has not been the project's strong point. Part of the reason for this has undoubtedly been the long period between the original preparation work and the final go-ahead. The protracted delays have stifled what involvement and commitment from local people originally existed.

Rather than trying to allocate blame for this delay, which is no doubt shared among the various parties involved, the emphasis now must be on the future. If the project is to achieve its objectives it must work out mechanisms to involve local people.

Significant Dates: EUCF, Tanzania

Late19[th] century: Large-scale clearing of forests in Usambaras begins.

1971: Main private logging company, Sikh Saw Mills (SSM), becomes a parastatal organisation and part of the Tanzania Wood Industries Corporation (TWICO).

1977: Inventory carried out by Finnish consulting company, Jaakko Pöyry, to ascertain commercial logging potential.
FINNIDA start supporting SSM logging.

1983: Second survey carried out by Jaakko Pöyry: logging area reduced by 5%.

1985: In response to increasing criticism, FINNIDA draw up plans for more detailed survey of the area: the Amani Forestry Inventory and Management Plan (AFIMP).

1986: International conference on tropical entomology formally protests against FINNIDA's support for logging activities.
SSM agree to stop logging in East Usambaras.

1988: The East Usambara Agricultural Development and Conservation (EUADEC) project launched by IUCN.
The AFIMP management plan finalised.
Discussions take place on the East Usambaras Catchment Forest Project (EUCF).

1990: Officials from IUCN and the Finnish National Board of Forestry meet to clarify the terms of cooperation between the EUADEC and EUCF projects.
EUCF project scheduled to start but is delayed.

1991: EUCF work in the field begins.

This will be no easy feat. There are clear conflicts of interest to be resolved. To conservationists, the East Usambaras are a treasure house of rare flora and fauna, and a steady source of water to the surrounding region. To pit-sawyers and Sikh Saw Mills, they are a timber gold mine ready to be exploited. To farmers and cardamom growers, they represent a basic source of income.

Methods of cultivation which are environmentally destructive will need to be changed if the project is to succeed. As Professor Omari of the University of Dar es Salaam sociology department points out, such changes seldom occur spontaneously, especially if there are other constraints, such as lack of access to credit, extension or other support services. Local communities, and individuals, also react differently. Their willingness to invest time, energy and funds in new schemes varies according to their income levels and the amount of land they own. Local cultural factors also play their part. Landowners in upland regions may lack the motivation to participate in watershed protection, since most of the benefits are reaped by those living downstream.

When it comes to extending the boundaries of forest reserves and restricting access to the forest, FINNIDA officials insist that every effort will be made to minimise the impact on local people. But villagers questioned were nevertheless concerned. Land hunger is so acute that few families will be prepared to give up their holdings easily; losing the income they earn from cardamom growing would also cause hardship. Although poorer households may be tempted by offers of cash compensation, the danger remains that such families will be forced to encroach on the forests again after these funds are exhausted. Indeed, according to Saidi Mbwana of the Ministry of Tourism, Natural Resources and Environment, the whole question of land tenure has to be properly addressed by FINNIDA and the Forest Department. The reality is that many rural inhabitants do not legally own the land they work. People with no title to land are unlikely to be motivated to invest time and energy in long-term forestry activities.

Although the project's planners are conscious of the danger of losing local support if they focus too heavily on policing duties, they have so far failed to address the issue of how they will involve local people in managing the forest or determining patterns of resource

Unless the project finds ways of reconciling forest protection with the needs of local people for fuel, fodder and land, the battle against encroachment will continue.

use. Local people felt strongly that they should play a role in drawing up any plans. As Miraji Shekoloa, secretary of Mikwinini village, pointed out to the Panos investigation team: "We are willing to assist in the establishment of buffer forests and to develop our own woodlots. However, we prefer to manage them ourselves. A security system developed by the local community is more effective than one brought from elsewhere."

Since the Forestry Division is the principal agency involved in implementing the project, developing effective communications between its staff and the local population will be a major priority. Forestry authorities will have to work hard to break down the barriers of mistrust that currently exist. The Forest Division recognises that new types of training will be needed. Forestry training in Tanzania has traditionally concentrated on technical aspects, such as how to organise forest patrols and combat pests and fires. What forestry staff have not been taught is how to work with local people in addressing issues of land use management, or how to transfer appropriate technology to rural communities.

Project planners will also have to recognise that forestry

development must embrace a broad spectrum of activities, with all the increased pressure on social services that this implies. When the EUCF project is fully implemented, basic services such as housing, medical facilities, transportation and education in the area will have to expand. These, in the long run, will prove instrumental in promoting sustainable forestry. There has to be a conscious realisation by governments and donor agencies such as FINNIDA that forestry development is not only about trees but also about people, specifically rural people. As Marcel Komanya, until recently Minister for Tourism, Natural Resources and Environment, has argued, forestry can be an effective tool for rural development, but only with the active involvement of local communities. This should not merely be some form of tokenism, but real and effective participation by local people in decisions which affect their daily lives.

Select Bibliography

Documents of the Ministry of Foreign Affairs, Finland

"Amani Forest Inventory and Management Plan Project", 1988

"East Usambara Catchment Forest Project: Project Document 1990-1993", February 1990

"Sikh Saw Mills (T) Ltd., Technical and Management Services Project Document", EKONO, August 1989

Pohjonen, Veli M., "East Usambara Catchment Forest Project: Appraisal of a Project Proposal and Project Document", November 1989

Documents of the International Union for the Conservation of Nature and Natural Resources (IUCN)

Hamilton, A., "East Usambaras Forest Inventory and Catchment Study Interim Report", October 1986

Hamilton, A. and Bensted-Smith, R. (Eds), "Forest Conservation in the East Usambara Mountains—Tanzania", 1989

Dasmann, R. F., "Ecological guidelines for balanced land use, conservation and development in high mountains", 1979

The Hill Forest Development Project, Nepal

This report was written by **Jan Sharma**, a journalist working on *The Independent* newspaper in Kathmandu, with the assistance of **Dr Keshar Man Bajracharya**, a consultant in forestry economics; **Bhuvan B Bajracharya** of the Centre for Economic Development and Administration, Tribhuvan University, Kathmandu; and **Shambu Manandhai**, photographer.

Grassroots and Green Hills

Resting on fresh bundles of fuelwood deposited beside the mountain trail, about a dozen women share filter-tipped cigarettes and ease their tired shoulders. As they wait for the rest of the convoy to arrive, they chat about the day's search for fuelwood.

"How late it is," says Kanchi Tamang anxiously. "We have to get home before dark." Tamang is 28 years old but looks 40, overworked and exhausted from the strain of supporting her family. Her husband, to whom she was married at 14, works as a clerk in Kathmandu. They have four children. "We have no kerosene in our village," she continued. "Some people went to the city and spent the whole day waiting in an endless queue. At the end of the day, they got only 2 litres of kerosene. But my husband says that he can no longer afford to pay for kerosene, and that how I cook the food is my business."

Her friend pulls a cigarette from her *patuka* (traditional waist pouch), and sighs. "It is easier to collect wood from the forest than wait the whole day for kerosene, especially when you have little money and it is so expensive." Catching and squashing a louse between her thumbnails, she adds: "These days it is hard to get wood from the forests. Ever since the government banned the felling of green trees, we have to spend the whole day searching for dead wood on the mountain slopes."

To the outsider, it is difficult to understand why Nepali women should have to work so hard to find fuel to cook the family meal, for Nepal seems blessed with endless mountain ranges covered in green vegetation. But much of that vegetation is scrub, and many of the country's forests have become thin and unproductive or have been cleared for agriculture. "Government officials say the people are responsible for destroying our forests. But how could we destroy the forests? We are dependent on them—we would die without forests," says Birkha Bahadur Nagarkoti, of Chakri village. "But we also need land to grow food."

Shambu Manandhai/Panos Pictures

Natural riches

Nepal is about the size of Bangladesh, occupying an area of 147,000 sq km between Tibet and India. The country has three ecological zones: the Terai, the hills and the mountains. Nearly half (45%) of the population live in the flat grasslands, cultivated fields and thick jungles of the Terai, which borders India. The hill areas are home to the majority (52%) of the population and since only a fraction of the land is cultivable, the area has the highest population density. The barren and snow-capped mountains bordering Tibet include the 8,848 metre Sagamartha (Mount Everest) and seven more of the world's tallest peaks.

The climate of this predominantly mountainous country spans the sub-tropical to the arctic. The vegetation ranges from subtropical hardwood forests in the Terai to tundra in the north, a treeless arctic region with frozen subsoil. In the mountains, towering ridges and swift icy rivers separate remote communities perched on steep valley slopes.

The variety of species in the natural forest reflects Nepal's diverse landscape and climate. The soil and vegetation also vary and in some areas bananas and apples ripen in the same season within kilometres of each other. In the hills, the main tree species are conifers (firs, spruce and blue pine) with some hardwoods such as oak, chestnut, alder, birch and poplar. In contrast, the Terai has mixed forests, comprised of the evergreen sal (*Shorea robusta*) and other broadleaved species such as the one known locally as *Sissoo (Dalbergia sissoo)*.

Geographic and climatic diversity are matched by ethnic diversity. More than 130 languages and dialects are spoken in Nepal. Most Nepalis (96%) live in villages, which are often no more than a scattered group of hamlets, comprising about 500 people. Travelling between hamlets may take several days of walking.

Once, these village communities managed the forest and agricultural land. For centuries Nepal consisted of no more than the Kathmandu valley; the rest of the country was made up of a number of small, autonomous principalities, tribal states and petty lordships. It was not until the eighteenth century, under Prithvi Narayan Shah,

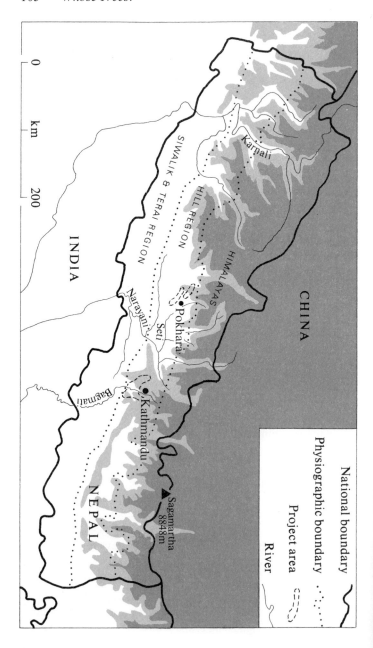

that the Himalayan region was unified into Nepal and a modern bureaucracy was developed.

Nepal's economy today remains agrarian, and most people scratch a living from subsistence agriculture, farming small plots of rice, wheat and barley. But difficult terrain and climate has limited the agricultural potential. The country boasts few natural resources, the most spectacular of which is the mountainous terrain. Those with most productive potential are the forests and the rivers. The latter has an almost untouched hydroelectric power potential of 83,000 megawatts—equal to that of the United States and Canada combined.

In contrast, forest resources have been overexploited, and the people of Nepal, particularly the women, face great difficulty in meeting the most basic of their energy needs: enough fuelwood to cook the daily meal.

Fuel for debate

1990 was a difficult year for Nepal. It experienced an unprecedented energy crisis after India refused to renew trade and transit treaties when they expired in March 1989. India closed all but two of its transit routes with Nepal. Supplies of salt, kerosene, petroleum products, medicine, baby food and other essentials began to dry up. At first, many Nepalis felt they could hold out against what they saw as a manifestation of Indian "dominance", but it soon became evident that they were David locked in battle with Goliath. Many feared New Delhi was attempting to annex Nepal in the way it had annexed the tiny kingdom of Sikkim in 1974.

Prices rocketed, industries began to close and agricultural production fell. The government had to remove its subsidy on kerosene, petrol and diesel, pushing the price of kerosene up from 6 rupees per litre (20 US cents) to 8.50 rupees (Rs). It appealed to the people to reduce consumption of kerosene in view of the uncertain supplies.

The energy crisis highlighted the problems of Nepal's landlocked economy and its dependence on its neighbours, particularly India. Attempts were made to find alternative energy sources and to increase Nepal's ability to meet domestic demand.

Shambu Manandhai/Panos Pictures

Nepal's energy problems were highlighted in 1990, after India had closed its trade routes with the landlocked kingdom. People queued for days for kerosene, but for most Nepalis fuelwood is their only source of energy.

In particular, there was much debate over the rate and implications of deforestation, for Nepal's forests provide the main source of energy for millions of rural Nepalis and an important source for urban areas. Fuelwood meets just over three-quarters of the energy needs of the economy; agricultural waste, dung, petroleum products, coal and electricity provide the rest. But most of this energy (95%) is used for cooking and heating.

The government claims that the dispute with India has accelerated the rate of deforestation to 240 hectares a day. However, a 1990 study, prepared by the Nepalese consulting agency New Era for the United States Agency for International Development (USAID), concluded that the recent dispute has increased forest loss by only 4.5 hectares a day.

Deforestation is often blamed for the downstream floods and landslides in India and Bangladesh. But geologists maintain that they are caused by the Himalayas' relative youth and geological instability. The Indian land-mass and the Tibetan plateau are moving towards one another, causing intermittent earthquakes and landslides and a gradual rise in mountain height. However, forest cover does help to absorb rainfall, alleviating the worst of the flooding, and to regulate water flow. Göran Haldin, a Finnish forestry advisor working for the Ministry of Forests and Soil Conservation, believes that deforestation seriously threatens the soil stability of Nepal's hillsides, where so many small farmers eke out a living.

Are the forests disappearing?

Some claim that there is a political element to the deforestation controversy, since forestry has attracted generous amounts of foreign aid to Nepal and it is to the advantage of some groups to make the most of deforestation so as to encourage donors to continue such funding. Yet part of the confusion clearly stems from the lack of reliable data. In 1979 the Nepal Community Forestry Development Project, under the FAO and World Bank cooperatives programme, estimated that accessible forests in the hills will have disappeared within 14 years and those in the Terai within 25 years. But these predictions are now viewed with scepticism by many donor agencies involved in Nepal's forest management. Forests are being degraded, they point out, rather than completely destroyed, and not at as fast a rate as was earlier predicted.

Reduced to patchy shrub with only a few mature trees still standing, degraded forests are not entirely worthless. Regeneration does take place but continued overcutting and grazing usually means that many trees fail to reach their full height and productivity is low. The main cause of outright deforestation is the spread of agricultural land, whereas overexploitation of the forests for fuelwood and fodder is responsible for their degradation, according to a study of land use changes in the Hill Forest Development Project area. Both are serious problems but "the cause of deforestation [land hunger] is to a great extent outside the control of the Ministry of Forests and Soil Conservation," says Tapio Leppänen, a Finnish forestry expert who has worked for several years on the Hill Forest Development Project.

Timber used to be a major export to India but the government has now outlawed wood exports. Previous attempts to prevent forest destruction have failed. In 1957 the government nationalised the forests, but the lack of effective protection and management only quickened their destruction. The Asian Development Bank (ADB) estimated in 1983 that between 35% and 40% of government forest land in Kathmandu and Pokhara districts was being encroached upon by farmers.

Although the Land Resources Mapping Project (LRMP) reported in 1979 that forest covered 38% of the land area, there has been no attempt to revise the forest land use maps to reflect the illegal clearing and encroachment of forest land. And many foresters and political leaders doubt the LRMP figures. "We do not actually *see* that much forest left in the country," says Dr Sanat Dhungel, district forest officer in Hetauda, who, like many, believes the extent of forest land and growing stock is overestimated.

While policymakers and academics continue to argue over the extent of forest encroachment and the most appropriate policy to halt it, attempts are being made at community level to manage the existing forest resources.

In many areas of Nepal, forests and pastures have been managed by traditional systems. The *kharka* system of the Sherpa people, for example, used a set of management practices and rules to protect and share fuelwood, timber, fodder and grasses. The Sherpas, who are illiterate, know exactly how many cattle can be supported on a particular *kharka* or grazing area. Many areas of healthy forest were also managed by religious or community trusts known as the *Guthi*.

Research into these traditional methods would help in the creation of official practices but they have never been studied. Instead, many traditional systems virtually collapsed after the government nationalised the forests and imposed alien forest management methods. One example of a state-imposed method was the *Talukdari* system devised by the Rana family rulers before they were ousted in 1951. This was, in fact, part of the state revenue administration. *Talukdars* were tax collectors. They controlled land and forest resources, not for management but for revenue purposes. Large chunks of forest were converted into farmland because of the attraction of higher income.

Community management of forests, however, continues. Throughout Nepal's hill area, small patches of forest are being regenerated. Many of the healthiest are those managed and owned by villagers, who know that their survival depends on their forest.

A happy marriage

"Look up there," says Chitra Bahadur Chetri, pointing to a developing forest in Hyangja, near Pokhara. "Ten years ago, that was a naked hill, so bare you could have seen a mouse move. Now it is becoming wooded. In a few years' time it could be so dense that even elephants will get lost."

In 1984, the villagers agreed not to use the forest area. The women, who collect most of the fuelwood and fodder, were asked to collect only dry wood. The cattle were prevented from entering the forest to protect young plants from being trampled and grazed. The result has been a remarkable regeneration.

The prosperity of Hyangja with its young forests is the talk of all the neighbouring villages. "If you find a bridegroom in Hyangja for your daughter, do not think twice about it," says Lal Bahadur, who lives nearby. "At worst, the bridegroom could always make a living by selling fuelwood from the forests. It is the right place to get your daughters married into," he advises.

Tek Bahadur Karki thinks the forest of Hyangja is a source of "pride for the villagers but envy for neighbours". What is his opinion of the forests that are beginning to grow in his village area? "Ours is such a baby. [The forest] is too young now for us to tell whether it will be handsome or ugly. But we are lucky to have a baby at all."

That the most effective strategy for Nepal as a whole is to rehabilitate existing resources rather than to create new plantations is something that the agencies and organisations involved in forestry aid have come to endorse. Rehabilitation can bring quicker results; it can also be sustainable, since it relies on the development of forest management skills in local communities rather than on imported plantation technology or expertise.

This conviction—that management of existing resources could well be the most cost-effective way of restoring forest cover—is the underlying philosophy of the Hill Forest Development Project (HFDP).

The Hill Forest Development Project

The HFDP was set up to help meet the fuelwood needs of the Kathmandu and Pokhara valleys, which consume 600,000 tonnes of wood a year, in tea shops, bakeries and restaurants, brickmaking and other industries, and in state institutions such as the army, the police and hospitals. Annual per capita consumption varies from 150 kg in the towns, where wood is supplemented by kerosene, liquefied petroleum gas and electricity, to 1,000 kg in some villages near forested areas. The average is 300 kg a year for the urban population and 600 kg in the rural areas. The position of the urban poor is particularly precarious. They are often unable to afford kerosene, and it is also difficult for them to collect wood locally.

The Nepal Fuelwood Corporation (now amalgamated with the Timber Corporation of Nepal) sells on average about 160,000 tonnes a year, obtained mainly from government forests in the Terai and Siwalik zones. It makes a healthy profit by paying a nominal royalty of Rs30 (US$1) per tonne to the Department of Forests and selling it at Rs550 (US$18) and Rs950 (US$32) in the Pokhara and Kathmandu valleys.

The bulk of the fuelwood is sold by poor families and traders who collect their supplies from the national forests. So the HFDP

Firewood on sale in Kathmandu; over three-quarters of the country's energy needs depend on fuelwood.

was seen as an important step towards rehabilitating considerable areas of forest and shrubland which, if properly managed, could then help meet the country's requirements. It was also seen as a vital step in protecting the Himalayan ecosystem.

Unspent budgets

The project was set up in 1984 after the Nepalese government asked the Asian Development Bank (ADB) to help fund a forestry project in the Kathmandu and Pokhara valleys. The ADB, however, insisted on a partner to the project after its appraisal team put together a package in the remarkably short time of three weeks. FINNIDA was then approached by the Nepalese government and agreed to pay US$1.4 million for training and technical assistance.

Originally the HFDP was costed at US$19.2 million over six years with about 30% consisting of foreign exchange costs. The ADB was to finance 87% of the cost, and the remainder was to be met by the Nepalese government.

The ADB approved a US$16.7 million loan in August 1983, repayable over 50 years at 1% interest. In the end, only US$3.2

HFDP Expenditure (in million US$)

Budget			
	Original budget	Actual spending	% of budget spent
Local Costs	13.7	2.5	18%
Foreign exchange costs	5.5	1.0	18%
Total	19.2	3.5	18%
Disbursements			
	Project contributions	Actual disbursements	% of funds disbursed
ADB	16.7	3.2	19%
Nepal	2.5	0.3	12%
Total	19.2	3.5	18%

million (19%) of the loan was disbursed. The balance is to be diverted into a proposed ADB programme loan to benefit other hill forestry projects.

The main reason for the massive underexpenditure was the reduction of HFDP's road construction programme and, to a lesser extent, the cancellation of the fencing programme and the fact that areas for pasture improvement had been greatly overestimated. These miscalculations occurred because the plans had been based on inaccurate information, something which did not come to light until an interim evaluation took place in 1986.

Foreign aid

The HFDP is one of several foreign-funded forestry projects in Nepal. Since 1977 the ADB has been funding the Sagarnath Forestry Project, which aims to establish 10,000 hectares of fast-growing fuelwood plantations on depleted forest land. The Karnali Bheri Integrated Development Project, funded by the Canadian International Development Agency (CIDA), plans to bring 783 hectares under forest cover. The Rapti Integrated Rural Development Project, supported by USAID, plans to turn 2,452 hectares into village fuelwood plantations. The Resources Conservation and Utilisation Project, also supported by USAID, had an afforestation component covering 3,320 hectares.

Swiss and German assistance is going towards the Tinau Watershed Integrated Development Project, which has an afforestation plan covering 142 hectares. The British government has provided technical assistance for research into protecting and improving degraded forests and shrubland.

FINNIDA has collaborated with many aid agencies in Nepal, and the government considers it the main agency for coordinating foreign assistance to forestry projects. From 1990, the government expects to receive an average of US$5-6 million per annum from FINNIDA.

Finnish aid has focused on strengthening forestry institutions to improve forestry management and has centred on training, the development of a forest resource information system and enhanced monitoring and evaluation procedures.

FINNIDA has also funded the integrated watershed management project in Kulekhani and Phewa Tal areas. The aim is to prevent the destruction of two lakes threatened by landslides and silt from the surrounding hillsides—the result of deforestation.

"There was a time when we thought the whole hill would slip down and end up as debris in the lake," says Laxmi Prasad Timilsinna, chairman of the local forest user committee. "Many of our neighbours moved out to the Terai. We no longer have to do this, because of the watershed project."

So far, this project has received strong support from the local people. Trilochan Sharma, an elderly villager and former *pradhan pancha* (village mayor) in Sarangkot, said he was so enthusiastic about the project that he had donated six ropanies (approximately one-third of a hectare) of steeply sloping land for pine plantations to protect the soil from imminent landslide. "Whenever I look at those plantations, I feel immense satisfaction," he said. "I may have lost a piece of property but I have saved much more of my own and others' land from sliding down into the lake."

Overall forest strategy

In 1957 the Nepalese government nationalised forests and in 1961 the Forest Act provided the first integrated forest legislation in Nepal.

Attempts to develop a comprehensive forestry strategy proved difficult. A National Forestry Plan (NFP) was formulated in 1971, which aimed:

- to attain self-sufficiency in fuelwood and fodder;
- to preserve and maintain the Terai forests in coordination with other land uses;
- to create community awareness to protect and maintain hill forests;
- to increase off-farm employment in the hills by diversifying forest activities;
- to preserve the existing gene pool of flora and fauna by creating national forest reserves.

With the Panchayat Protected Forest Rules of 1978, the government aimed to hand nationalised forest back to local communities. This idea received strong backing from the World Bank but the NFP was never implemented and there is now concern that the most recent Master Plan for the forestry sector—prepared by the ADB, FINNIDA and the Nepalese government at the cost of US$1.8 million and approved by the cabinet in April 1989—may share a similar fate. The Master Plan attempts to provide an overall perspective within which different forestry and forestry-related activities can be developed in complementary ways. Critics say it takes too narrow a view of forestry and fails to address the fundamental problem of land resource management.

FINNIDA remains optimistic. Heikki Rissanen, a FINNIDA forestry advisor, says: "There is a political commitment and an explicit statement at ministerial level of intent to implement the Master Plan. We agree that the Plan has some shortcomings but nevertheless it is promising. It outlines practical, tangible programmes for which it has calculated the costs and level of financial and technical support necessary—from outside sources and as well from the government." He added: "The most important thing is that the Master Plan has secured a political commitment to forestry from those responsible for channelling the resources. It may not be implemented exactly as planned but it has helped to formulate good policies. Anyway, such large-scale plans are not meant to be static; they have to be constantly reviewed and revised."

The government has ordered a review of the Master Plan because the political events of 1990, when the government re-introduced a multi-party system, may affect certain aspects of implementation but no substantial policy changes are anticipated.

Rissanen stressed that the important point is that the Master Plan has correctly identified the core problem—the gap between supply and demand of forest produce. "It may be that the initial targets are unrealistic but figures can be revised. The point is that more forest products are being produced than before and the trend of demand exceeding supply is being reduced. We hope eventually to reverse that trend. If the Plan succeeds in directing resources towards the right solutions, then it is achieving its purpose."

Blueprint for recovery: the HFDP

The HFDP brief was to work on the hill forests at Thankot, Tikabhairav and Godavari villages in the Kathmandu valley, and Aushadhi Ban and Nirmal Pokhara forests divisions in the Pokhara valley. The valleys are catchment areas for the Bagmati and Seti rivers, and improved hill forests would enhance their water catchment properties.

The Kathmandu forests, estimated to cover about 22,000 hectares, lie between 1,200 metres and 2,170 metres. Annual rainfall ranges between 1,259 mm and 2,051 mm. The Pokhara forest lies between 900 metres and 1,600 metres, with an average rainfall of 3,707 mm. The HFDP was projected to cover about 5,000 hectares, in areas where the average farm holding is 0.5 hectares.

The Department of Forests, within the Ministry of Forests and Soil Conservation, was to be the main executing agency and the project would be implemented by a project manager appointed by the government. Coordinators were to be a committee of representatives from the Ministry of Finance, the Departments of Roads and of Livestock Development, the general manager of the Fuelwood Corporation of Nepal and the Chief Conservator of Forests, as well as the conservator of forests for the project areas.

The project's aim was to "rely heavily on the recuperative qualities of natural Himalayan forests, aided by timber stand improvement and forest protection". According to the 1983 ADB appraisal: "Forest improvement and protection...is considered the most effective and the cheapest way to improve the depleted hill forests of Nepal and bring them under sustained production."

It would also act as a catalyst by developing professional skills

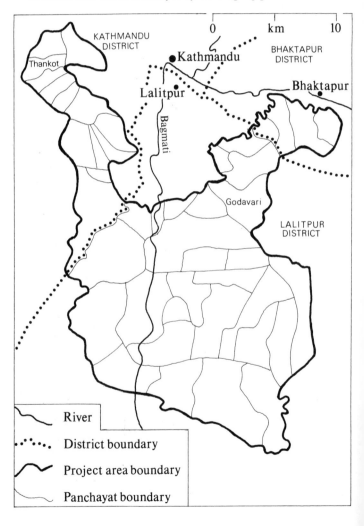

and a permanent institution within the Department of Forests. To ensure sustained production of fuelwood and fodder, the HFDP planned to plant fast-growing species.

The key elements of the strategy were:
● Timber stand improvement
● Shrubland tending
● Harvesting and utilisation of forest products
● Planting of mixed fuelwood and fodder species
● Training

To facilitate effective management and fuelwood transportation, forest roads and trails were to be constructed; the aim was to build 104 km of new roads and upgrade 55 km of existing ones. A new forest engineering division was to be created to do this.

A forest inventory was also to be carried out in the additional areas of Dhading, Makwanpur and Syanja, complementing an earlier study which had assessed the quality and composition of different tree species, leaf fodder and fuelwood.

Timber stand improvement (TSI), in which forests are carefully managed so that their composition and quality are improved, was to be carried out in 7,000 hectares of forest area. Another 16,000 hectares of shrubland were also to be tended to stimulate natural regrowth of the forests. The project also planned to plant mixed fuelwood and fodder species in 4,000 hectares, as well as to improve 1,500 hectares of pasture land. Within an area of 1,600 hectares, where patches of natural forest already existed, extra planting was to take place to improve its quality. Fencing was to be undertaken where necessary.

Existing forestry institutions in the project area were to be strengthened not only through the provision of vehicles, equipment and additional staff, but also through training for about 1,000 staff, in Nepal as well as abroad. This would be complemented by foreign and local consultancy services.

The project designers anticipated that the most likely stumbling blocks would be the lack of implementation experience in scientific forest management, the illegal removal of forest products and uncontrolled grazing. They advised minimising these risks by locating the project in those forest divisions with the strongest organisational support, by providing consultants to implement the

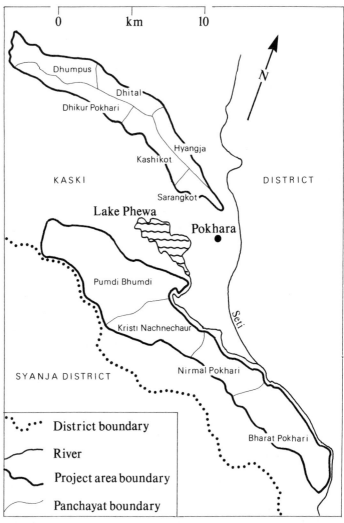

HFDP and by diversifying silvicultural works. To discourage illegal grazing, they suggested fencing, the hiring of *ban heralu* (forest watchers) from among the villagers and the establishment of a mechanism through which villagers could share forest products.

Grassroots interests

The *panchayat* system was introduced by King Mahendra in 1962, when he outlawed political parties. Each village *panchayat* consists of a group of hamlets with a population of no more than 500. *Panchayats* are subdivided into wards, which comprise two or three hamlets. One *panchayat* might have as many as nine or 11 wards. This highly stratified system dominated local activities and organisation until April 1990, when intense public pressure resulted in the re-introduction of multi-party democracy. *Panchayats* are now more usually termed village development committees.

Informal self-help groups or community associations are often found at village level and, with training, these can become effective "user" groups with authority over local forest resources. Under the pre-April 1990 political structure, the government had approved but never fully implemented a decentralisation scheme. It called for the formalisation of user groups, as a means of mobilising villagers to implement district-level projects like the HFDP.

User groups usually consist of seven members, mostly from the high caste groups of Brahmins and Chetries. In one case in Hyangja, people belonging to lower, occupational caste groups, such as blacksmiths, were systematically discouraged from becoming members simply because their requirements from the forest, mainly fuelwood, were likely to be much higher than their contribution. Most user groups represent about 100 households.

The group members are responsible for mobilising people to maintain and protect the forests, and for resolving conflicts. They also collect each household's contribution, in cash or kind, towards paying the *ban heralu*, as well as the *katuwal*, who is traditionally responsible for disseminating information in the villages.

Under the decentralisation scheme, greater autonomy and decisionmaking powers were to be given to user groups at ward level, the basic unit of the *panchayat* political hierarchy. In reality, however, there was little change to the way authority was exercised. District Forest Officers (DFOs) continued to decide who were members of the user groups and who led them, often choosing the ward chairman as leader. Thus ward chairmen, who had originally often been handpicked by the DFOs, were regarded as part of the political regime rather than representative of grassroots' interests.

Waking up from the dream

An interim evaluation of the project's progress was carried out in 1986, and its findings were a shock.

The problems lay in the project document itself. Nepali forestry officials say that the statistics upon which the project's ambitious dream had been based were wrong. "It was an example of textbook management with no base in reality," says Kapil Chitrakar, former chief of the HFDP and now head of the Community Forestry Project. "The plan had several drawbacks and was very poorly developed and designed. All estimates were badly done. A setback was inevitable. This is why we have never been able to spend the money."

The review revealed a catalogue of miscalculations. For example, an inventory showed that there was only two-thirds of the original estimate of shrubland—and there was just 610 hectares of grassland, instead of the original estimate of 7,000 hectares.

The review also showed that there was no large fuelwood surplus as originally believed. It had been assumed that only 20% of fuelwood produced in the project area would be required locally and that the rest would be available to meet urban needs. In fact, local demand far exceeded supply. The 10 backloads of fuelwood (each between 20 kg and 30 kg) available annually for each family in the project area lasts on average for one month. The deficit is made up with animal dung and other residues. And the estimates had not taken account of local needs for additional logs and poles for huts and cattlesheds.

The development of new forest management practices and their implementation was proving to be far more complicated and time-consuming than anticipated. And although it was a government-initiated project, a state ban on felling green trees delayed the implementation of the key objective: timber stand improvement (TSI).

The road construction plan—the most expensive part of the project—was found to be unrealistic by HFDP experts, who recommended the cheaper option of constructing and maintaining forest trails. The target of creating 104 km of new roads and

Shambu Manandhai/Panos Pictures

The steep valleys of Nepal are especially vulnerable to the effects of deforestation: soil erosion, floods and landslides.

upgrading 55 km of existing roads had been calculated on the basis of an inadequate small-scale map of the project area. The idea that the Forest Department, rather than the Roads Department, carry out road building was misguided since mountain roads need engineers who know of the dangers of soil erosion and landslides.

And although the project document had anticipated a lack of skilled manpower, the real problem was that existing staff were too overworked with their normal forest duties to devote particular attention to HFDP activities.

A complex web

There are a number of reasons why the original project document, prepared by the ADB appraisal mission, was inadequate. Dipak Gyawali, an engineer who heads an energy consulting group, thinks it is symptomatic of the problem of lobbying for foreign aid. Although Nepal has a vast forest potential, it earns its foreign income not by exporting forest products but by lobbying for more aid in the name of its forest sector. "People are rewarded for pushing projects," he points out. A western consultant based in Kathmandu believes that the large amounts of money invested in aid projects attract interests which undermine efficient project design and implementation: "Any time there is a contract, people come sniffing around to get some of it."

A related factor in this instance was the fact that the ADB authorities wanted to push the loan agreement through quickly. So the Nepalese government, the ADB and FINNIDA all went ahead with a document that had been hastily compiled on the basis of quite inadequate data, because of administrative and financial imperatives.

Another hindrance was the reform of the organisational structure of the Department of Forests, the executing agency for the project. The department head, previously the Chief Conservator of Forests, is now called Director General, assisted by four deputy directors in charge of forest development, administration, management and utilisation. The forestry sector was formerly divided into nine territorial circles following the Indian pattern. Now Nepal is divided into five development regions, in turn split into 14 zones, and further subdivided into 75 districts, each headed by a DFO. The next unit is the village *panchayat*, of which there are about 3,000.

Such reorganisations inevitably entail a period of confusion and adjustment, which delay decisionmaking and implementation. And the changes do not appear to have halted the frequent transfer of officials, including DFOs, which has been a major hindrance to the execution of projects, sometimes resulting in the loss of a year's working time. This lack of continuity in staff, combined with the low motivation endemic in government bureaucracies, has badly affected the pace of HFDP's implementation.

HFDP: The revised plan

These setbacks and changes forced a comprehensive review of the project. Targets were revised and a new plan of operation prepared by 1988. The road programme was dramatically scaled down, although even those reduced targets were never reached (see box on p124). The plan to improve pasture areas and grow grasses and legumes for cattle was dropped since only 610 hectares of grassland existed.

Training activities

It became clear that training was more important than had been realised and so training plans were increased. Many of the forest management techniques were new to the hill areas of Nepal, and some systems had to be tested and standardised before training could even begin.

By the end of the project in 1990 a total of 1,275 people—forestry staff as well as village leaders and members of forest user groups—had received training. Seppo Hämäläinen, managing director of Silvestria, a Finnish consultancy firm which provided technical assistance to HFDP, commented that, "We exceeded the original target of 1,000 people because it went so well, and it was clearly much better to get more people trained than more hectares planted." Time spent on short-term training studies abroad was also exceeded, and four students undertook MScs abroad.

Towards the end of the project, FINNIDA provided demonstrations and training in forest harvesting and management using appropriate tools. This was possible because the training budget was channelled directly by FINNIDA to the project, thus

Project extension activities included the development of improved tools and techniques for cutting fodder and firewood which cause less damage to living wood.

avoiding the kind of funding delays which had hindered earlier implementation of forestry training and techniques.

HFDP Targets

	Shrubland Management	TSI	Plantation (Afforestation)
Original Target	16,000 ha	7,000 ha	4,000 ha
Revised Target	5,067 ha	2,310 ha	3,127 ha
Achieved	3,471 ha	1,050 ha	2,500 ha
	Roads	**Trails**	**Training**
Original Target	105 km	55 km	68 months
Revised Target	22 km	30 km	
Achieved	10 km	15 km	72 months

Hämäläinen explained why this aspect of training was important: "We believed that the collection of firewood and the making and maintenance of forest trails needed better tools—to make an easier, cleaner cut and cause less damage to the living wood, for instance. This entailed a slight adaptation of traditional tools. We started a bit too late in the project's life but there is a lot of scope for developing good management methods using local skilled labour, including blacksmiths who make the improved tools."

FINNIDA plan to continue this activity in the next phase of their forestry assistance to Nepal—the Forest Management, Utilisation and Development Project (FMUDP), which FINNIDA and the government of Nepal have agreed should run from 1991-1994.

Publicity

The revised 1988 plan of operation incorporated new activities to increase public awareness of forest legislation, management and silvicultural techniques via the mass media. These included the publication and distribution of a forestry newsletter called *Kalpabrichhya* (Sanskrit name for a mythical tree that gives any fruit one desires), the broadcasting of a weekly radio programme *Ban Batika* (the forest garden) and the production of films and video programmes. The radio programme is under way but because there is immense competition for the prime time evening slot, it goes out in the morning when villagers are working. The newsletter and videos have not yet materialised and there is considerable uncertainty about how effective they will be. FINNIDA's forestry advisor Heikki Rissanen believes that "the only way to really reach the villagers is through the practical work—the training events."

Plantations

Plantations of indigenous and fast-growing species, useful for fuelwood and fodder, were planned in small, open patches where trees currently do not regenerate. These include black locust *(Robinia pseudoacacia)*, a fast-growing tree which sends out a multitude of new suckers from its horizontal roots and is a particularly effective anchor for shifting soils, and black wattle *(Acacia mearnsii)* for fuelwood. White mulberry *(Morus alba)* and ash *(Fraxinus floribunda)*, known locally as *kimbu* and *lankuri* respectively, are grown for fodder. Alder, known locally as *utis*, which is native to the Himalayas and grows extensively in the hills of northern India and in Nepal, has also been planted.

Fourteen nurseries, each with an average capacity of 500,000 polybag seedlings per year, were to be set up under the HFDP. The original afforestation target was 4,000 hectares but this was scaled down to 3,127 hectares in 1988.

Shrubland management

One of HFDP's principal tasks is to manage the 27,000 hectares of hill forest. The general management plan was complete in 1987 but the detailed working plans were not ready until 1989. Based on the forest inventory and the HFDP's demand and supply projections, they described the forest types and the management options, and included detailed annual treatment and harvest times for each forest compartment.

The success of the shrubland improvement programme has proved a breakthrough in hill forest management. Shrubland is usually forest land which has been overexploited and has lost most of its tree cover. By taking out undesirable species and weeds, the degraded land slowly recovers and trees begin to regenerate naturally. For a given area, shrubland management requires only a quarter of the costs of establishing new plantations.

"Shrubland management is a more effective and beneficial strategy than solely planting new trees," says Gorän Haldin, Finnish forestry advisor in Kathmandu. "The lesson is that we need to take care of what already exists, instead of concentrating on creating new things."

Shrubland improvement work was ultimately carried out on 3,471 hectares, instead of the original target of 16,000 hectares. This slow progress was due to delays in the recruitment of staff and the testing of silvicultural procedures. Furthermore, the Finance Ministry released the budget in December, instead of July, after the peak demand time for leaf fodder and when district staff had been assigned to more urgent duties than the HFDP activities. In effect, funds were not available in the field until February or March.

Timber stand improvement

Timber stand improvement (TSI) got off to a particularly slow start but proved to be a successful approach to hill forest management, eventually covering 1,050 hectares, compared with the original target of 7,000 hectares. The original plans took no account of the government ban on cutting green trees, imposed at the end of the 1970s. TSI improves the composition and quality of unproductive forests by removing dead, dying and diseased trees and felling older, unproductive trees and some young trees to open out the forest canopy and stimulate regeneration. So it directly contravened government forest legislation.

TSI was due to start in 1985 but the government delayed approval until May 1989, when it eventually changed the relevant legislation. The Ministry of Forest and Soil Conservation in effect took almost five years to approve the TSI norms prepared by the project. Since the law already provided for exceptions, the government seems to have deliberately concentrated on the letter rather than the spirit of the law.

However, once TSI began, the government was so impressed with this approach that it decided to use it in all forests, whether or not they are under HFDP management. In this sense, the TSI operation ushered in a new, if delayed, era in Nepal's hill forest management.

Supply and demand

Although the HFDP was set up specifically to provide forest products, its impact so far on fuelwood and fodder supplies has been marginal. There are various reasons for this. According to Tapio Leppänen, the main one is that "the Forest Department simply did not have the capacity to launch forest management operations on a large enough scale". He explained: "First, appropriate management systems must be created and tested. Second, the staff must be trained. Third, local needs must be incorporated throughout the entire process. Realistically, the project could only be expected to reach the stage of initial development and testing....It is understandable that changes in traditional working methods cannot be achieved in the relatively short period of the project, especially in a large organisation such as the Department of Forests."

Another factor was the inaccuracy of the original projections. The project areas are densely populated; between 1971 and 1981, the population in rural areas increased by 20% and that in the towns by 40%. It became clear that even if the 12,000 hectares of the HFDP forest was fully productive—yielding the maximum of 10 tonnes of fuelwood per hectare per year—it would still account for less than a quarter of total consumption. The situation was further complicated by the discrepancy between the targeted areas and the areas actually covered by the HFDP's TSI activities. And since the stock is still building up, only a fraction of the potential yield (estimated to be one or two tonnes per hectare per year) is being extracted for fuelwood.

The HFDP areas of shrubland are beginning to produce fuelwood. New plantations have been created in 2,500 hectares and replanting undertaken in another 2,700 hectares. At present the contribution of these areas to meeting fuelwood and fodder needs is small. All these activities need to be supported by tree growing in homesteads and on farmland, by popularising improved fuel-efficient stoves, and by the use of alternative energy sources such as biogas and solar, although the latter are still too expensive for widespread use.

However, the HFDP forests and shrublands are responding well to silvicultural treatment and management. The lower mixed hardwood forests, between 1,000 metres and 2,000 metres, have become dense and luxuriant as a result of only a few years' management and protection, especially in the Pokhara valley where it rains heavily. Such increases in tree cover do also seem to have significantly reduced soil erosion. No hard data exist but some officials believe that soil loss in the most degraded areas could have been reduced by 90%.

These degraded forests could achieve full crown cover, averaging 150 cubic metres to 200 cubic metres of wood biomass per hectare within a decade, as happened in two forest areas, the Aushadhi Ban and Rani Ban, in the Pokhara valley. Apart from the fuelwood such forests produce, some sections could subsequently yield good quality construction timber from mature trees left during the process of TSI. Depending upon availability and demand, managed and protected forests in the project area could yield Rs2,000 (US$67) or more per hectare annually, according to Dr Keshar Man Bajracharya.

The sustainability of any such achievements depends on continued hill forest management, a process which can be maintained only with the active involvement of local communities and their grassroots structures. Yet it is in this area of community participation that the HFDP has been at its weakest. Finnish expert Tapio Leppänen defended the project's reputation: "All projects in Nepal are in a similar position over this. And considering the HFDP's role in the overall national forestry programme, it could be said that it has strongly promoted social forestry."

People power

The HFDP operates within the same districts as the Community Forestry Development Project (CFDP). The CFDP hands over forests to local communities and supports them in the management of these forests, while the HFDP manages the forests not yet transferred to the local communities. The revised 1988 plan stated that "the HFDP should not hinder the expansion of community forestry. When a community is ready to take over the management

Sean Sprague/Panos Pictures

Some project activities have been criticised for paying lip-service to the idea of involving villagers. Effective community participation has also been hampered by Nepal's centralised political structure, now undergoing changes after the pro-democracy demonstrations of 1990.

of a certain area managed under the HFDP, the district forest controller should hand it over to the community."

"In reality," says Leppänen, "most of the forests where the project operated were potential community forests and were not designated to remain national forests." He disputes the view that local people's dependence on these forests was not taken into account by HFDP and that community involvement was not properly planned for. However, he and FINNIDA officials agree that finding the right mechanisms to involve villagers and user groups has been extremely difficult.

Ram Paudyal, the district forest officer in Pokhara, says: "All forests are community forests. Without community support and participation, nothing can be done." In practice, however, the participation of villagers is often sought only as a last resort, and then mainly to help in protecting the forests.

All important decisions—schedules for thinning and pruning, the establishment of plantations and the tree species, target planning and financial outlay—are taken by government officials in

Kathmandu who lack field experience. Workers in the field and user groups were often only consulted when the project had to hire villagers to carry out activities.

The whole issue of participation seems to have been approached largely from the negative angle of anticipated illegal removal of forest products and uncontrolled livestock grazing. The HFDP is not alone in this attitude.

When the *panchayat* system was dissolved in April 1990 and the multi-party system revived, the user groups were thrown into disarray and loyalties were split. Had the user groups been considered genuinely representative of the communities' forest concerns, they might have survived the political upheaval. But the ward chairmen were seen as symbols of authority from above, not of people's concerns at the grassroots.

Will the new user groups include members of all political parties or will they be dominated by followers of the largest party? Disputes have already begun. "We do not know what the future looks like in terms of organisational management," says Gokul Raj Pandey, regional forest director in Pokhara.

The user group system was essentially a bureaucratic version of community participation and tied non-political activities to the ups and downs of political priorities. The effect of this arrangement was demonstrated by the confusion which followed the collapse of the *Panchayat* system. The resulting disorder has given some people an opportunity to remove forest products, according to the Hyangja and the Sarangkot forest user groups. Uncertainty over the groups' status and function has also led to confusion over the position of the forest watchers and how they should be paid, which has in turn undermined their commitment.

FINNIDA officials point out that many of the factors just described reflect Nepal's political structure and its highly stratified social organisation, and as such are outside the control of a development agency. But they have major implications for the success of community participation and should have been understood and acknowledged in the HFDP plans.

Not all HFDP forests have user groups, and not all groups follow the same procedures. Their management has not been very effective, partly because of their uncertain relationship with the forest office which sees them principally as protectors. User groups have to agree management procedures with the local DFOs, who have their own priorities.

The user groups need to be much more effective, and their areas of supervision and control need to be clearly defined. In Dhikur Pokhari and in Hyangja, there are disputes over the demarcation of controls between different villages. So far, such disputes have not had any destructive effects, as the forests are well protected. But once controlled use and development of the forests begins, such disagreements could become serious. There will have to be arrangements for arbitration, and the forest office may have to play an important role, as local representatives are likely to follow group or caste interests. "This is very probable," commented Tapio Leppänen. "Nevertheless, it is a political problem and so outside the field of interest of the Ministry."

Local involvement in managing forests is essential because it is these communities which bear the brunt of deforestation. Villagers are aware of the importance of forests in maintaining environmental stability. Some believe that the HFDP failed to address people's involvement because it concentrated more on the idea of who owns the forest than who uses it, and because project staff were working on government land and so did not regard community involvement as their concern.

Sharing the forest

Another key issue yet to be properly addressed is the lack of a standard benefit-sharing mechanism. Villagers are allowed to collect foliage and dead wood, but there are different arrangements within communities for sharing forest products among user-households. In some cases, a household is allowed to collect as much foliage and dead wood as it can but only on certain days. In other areas, each household is allowed to collect a set amount each year—for example, 400 kg to 500 kg.

In the HFDP forests in Pokhara, user groups are involved in thinning and pruning, and are allowed to take the cut foliage, as well as dry and dead wood. In some cases, each household is allowed one backload of forest products. In Godavari district, there is no system of benefit-sharing and, as a result, thinning and pruning have not yet been completed. The need to strike a balance between contributing labour and sharing the benefits will become more urgent once TSI becomes more widely established. A consistent and workable system will be important to the sustained commercial use of the forests. "There have been promising efforts in the past to control forest utilisation in collaboration with the local people and the [Forest] Department. Yet often these efforts have petered out within a couple of years because of a change in local administration or Department personnel," commented Leppänen.

Conclusion

The serene silence of many of Nepal's valleys is often broken by the familiar and insistent sound of someone using a *bancharo* (a metal implement) to chop down trees up in the hills. "Hey, who's up there?" shouts the forest guard. "These people go anywhere. They think they can outwit me. I can't run after all of them, all the time." He pauses and then adds: "But there has not been as much destruction in recent years. Nevertheless, some people are very poor and they can only earn a living by making charcoal."

The process of encroachment into forests in the hill areas of Nepal is a complex phenomenon. It is rooted in the needs of village communities for fuel and fodder. "We are always troubled by forest officials. But we are not destroying forests. We only collect *daura* [wood] to cook food. How else could we keep the fire burning in our *chulo* [stove]. What is wrong with collecting *daura*?" asks one village woman. Families use forest products to satisfy their basic needs. But these short-term needs have to be balanced with the long-term preservation of the resources.

The officials' case is not helped when villagers see government-sponsored activities being implemented before their eyes which seem to contradict everything they have been told.

For example, the villagers in Godavari, Kathmandu division, object to the large-scale stone and marble quarrying now under way. "People from the forest office tell us not to destroy trees because otherwise there will be no forest today and no mountains tomorrow. But then why are they destroying the mountains by blasting them?" one woman complained. Quarrying reportedly increased at the end

Quarrying at Godavari, Kathmandu valley. Trees have to compete with other claims on the land, such as agriculture and mining. Many argue that Nepal's forestry Master Plan takes too narrow a view of land resource management and thus has limited chances of success.

of 1990, because of a fear that the interim government might call a halt to the practice. The Phulchoki hills, a renowned sanctuary for at least 300 species of birds, is slowly being dynamited into an open-pit moonscape, accelerating the destruction of the last remaining virgin forest in the Kathmandu valley.

The activities in Godavari highlight a key problem: the absence of clearly thought-out, sustainable projects and programmes which address the development priorities of Nepal. Although Tapio Leppänen says that "it was realised from the very beginning that rural communities were to be the primary beneficiaries of the HFDP," some feel that it was conceived largely as an attempt to meet urban needs. Yet one aim of any forest policy should be to meet the needs of rural communities. Forests are being destroyed by people not out of apathy or stupidity, but because of the need for fuel, fodder and land. They are claiming forest land to grow food.

Successful management of hill forests will remain a dream as long as abject poverty continues to make people dependent on land and forest resources. "It is the pervasive poverty that compels people to exploit natural resources so intensively," says Dr Harka

Gurung, an eminent scholar and former minister. Successive governments in Nepal have failed to address the issue of land hunger. Forest management is more than a technical affair; it is a tricky political process of land use management. Government policy, not the poor, should be blamed for forest destruction.

The project illustrates that it is not foreign aid Nepal needs, but effective management of forest resources and adequate reinvestment of the revenue earned. Part of this revenue could then go towards building up community projects which benefit villagers and so ensure their continued cooperation. Heikki Rissanen of FINNIDA has a more positive view and feels that foreign aid and effective management are not mutually exclusive: "Foreign aid can indeed play a significant role in establishing effective management practices— and the HFDP has illustrated this."

Significant Dates: HFDP, Nepal

1957: Nepalese government nationalises forests.

1961: Forest Act: first legislation on forests.

1962: Panchayat system introduced by King Mahendra.

1967: Forest Protection Act.

1970: Forest Products (Sales and Distribution) Rules - government bans cutting of green trees.

1971: National Forestry Plan formulated.

1983: August - Asian Development Bank approves funding for Hill Forest Development Project (HFDP). FINNIDA become partners.
December - agreement for project and funding signed.

1984: HFDP starts.

1986: Interim inventory and evaluation of HFDP.

1987: Following HFDP evaluation, general management plan revised.

1988: Revised HFDP targets and additional extension activities established.
Master Plan for forestry sector developed by government, Asian Development Bank and FINNIDA.

1989: Following changes in government legislation, timber stand improvement begins (originally scheduled for 1985).

1990: April - Re-introduction of multi-party system.
July - HFDP formally ends.

1991-94: Forest Management, Utilisation and Development Project .

"Teaching a dog to sit on a chair"

One lesson to be drawn from the HFDP's experience is that institutional strengthening has to go beyond the reinforcement of existing bureaucracies. It must change the entire orientation of the Department of Forestry. Forests continue to be seen primarily as a source of revenue to the government, and the Department has always played the role of policeman. "Changing that orientation is tantamount to teaching a dog how to sit on a chair properly—not easy," one official said.

Interference from the Ministry undermined the authority of the Department of Forests and the project management, and created obstacles instead of smoothing out bureaucratic problems. The Ministry often arbitrarily hired or transferred employees in the project, and overruled the authority of the project or Department over the choice of staff for training abroad. Field officers, even at district level, were kept away from the planning and implementation of the project's programmes. The government delayed the deployment of staff, the release of certain budgets and the implementation of TSI by dragging its feet over legislative issues.

The HFDP correctly identified fuelwood and fodder as the basic needs of Nepalese rural society. The act of collecting fuelwood, even within community forests, often means healthy trees are poached or their branches cut in a way that hinders their proper growth. This process will undoubtedly lead to the destruction of forests unless there is regular and efficient forest management, combined with the planting of some fast-growing species. This is the approach which the project aimed to promote.

Managing nature

Six years after its launch, the HFDP's targets have not been met but its philosophy is undoubtedly important: that the scientific management of hill forests is the most cost-effective and sustainable way of halting deforestation and producing fuelwood and fodder.

A crucial lesson to emerge from this study is the importance of gaining community support and establishing realistic mechanisms to involve people in the practical management of hill forests. Tapio Leppänen says: "The policy should be to complement the community forestry programme in promoting development in that direction. The activities should be implemented in such a way that they can be sustained by the local consumers whenever it is likely that the area in question will be handed over to a user group."

The critical problem is the demarcation between national and community forests, and the integration of authority and responsibility between the different government agencies involved in forestry. "What is required is to transfer ownership to the village community," argues Krishna Kumar Panday of the International Centre for Integrated Mountain Development (ICIMOD) in Kathmandu. "Community forests are defined as national forest and thus brought under the district forest officer. This is exactly where the problem lies. What we need is a denationalisation of the legislation in order to allow community forestry, pure and simple."

Göran Haldin, FINNIDA forestry programme advisor, disagrees, believing that the question of forest ownership is extremely complex: "Joint legal ownership of the forest is no more likely to work in Nepal than anywhere else. Arguing for joint ownership of the forest by villages is inviting political trouble, a legal mess and even fighting—as has been the case with land ownership. Developing user rights is the best approach."

Although the involvement of communities has been incomplete, local people do have a general sense of achievement about the progress so far. They are proud that they have contributed to the improvement of the forests. Because of their efforts in controlling overexploitation, the trees have grown back, and there are forests once again. Undoubtedly, they would have felt more pride had they been associated with all aspects of planning, implementation, and monitoring and evaluation of the work.

The growth of the forests shows that the people are cooperating with the government's restrictions on forest use. In order to sustain this activity after the project's end, the management capability of the user groups needs to be strengthened.

The issue of community involvement is certainly a complex one. Although many non-governmental organisations have been active in Nepal, identifying genuine user groups has not been easy. There is hope that the recent move towards democracy in the country could generate an upsurge in community participation in all aspects of life.

Since the revival of multi-party democracy in April 1990, the dominant Nepali Congress and various factions of the Nepal Communist Party have been taking an active part in conservation and the protection of forest resources.

Looking to the future

The HFDP ended on 15 July 1990, but its activities will continue under a new Forest Management and Utilisation Development Project (FMUDP). The outcome of an agreement between the government of Nepal and FINNIDA, FMUDP is scheduled to last from 1991 to 1994 and is essentially a follow-up to the HFDP. It aims to develop, disseminate and institutionalise forest management planning in a national and leasehold forestry programme. It also aims to introduce appropriate management and utilisation techniques for different types of forests, and to develop appropriate tools and transfer technology as a way of stimulating wider socio-economic development. Like the HFDP, it aims to increase the sustainable productivity of forests and to protect the forest ecosystem from degradation.

It is too early to say what this project will bring the people of Nepal. What is certain is that there is a genuine attempt not to repeat the mistakes of the HFDP. A number of pilot areas representing different forest types, ecological and social conditions are to be set up as testing grounds for the project. The Ministry officials involved in the FMUDP say they will work in close cooperation with other forestry projects, such as the Community Forestry Programme.

Yet there remains the difficulty of finding effective mechanisms to incorporate local involvement in the management and development of forestry. It is evident that unless local people have clearly defined user rights to manage the forests for their own benefit, there can be little prospect of effective community participation. For this it is vital to develop trust and confidence between the people and the government. The prospects for sustainable forestry may have a better chance with the return to democracy, but there is certainly a long way to go.

Select Bibliography

Documents of the Ministry of Foreign Affairs, Finland

"Revised Plan of Operation for the Hill Forest Development Project for the period 1989-June 1990", September 1988

"Hill Forest Development Project — FINNIDA/FINNEP — Environmental impact assessment of Sarangkot road, Pokhara", April 1990

"Contribution of the government of Finland to the Hill Forest Development Project—Extension Phase—January 1989-June 1990"

Leppänen, Tapio, "Assessment of the Hill Forest Development Project (July 1984-June 1990)", May 1990

Leppänen, Tapio, "In-service Training and Extension in the Hill Forest Development Project (July 1984-June 1990)", May 1990

Documents of the Asian Development Bank (ADB)

"Appraisal of the Hill Forest Development Project in the Kingdom of Nepal", June 1983

"Nepal: Hill Forest Development Project (Loan No.633-NEP(SF)), Project Completion Review", June 1990

Other Sources

Thapa, Gopal B. and Weber, Karl E., "Population and Environment in the Hills of Nepal", *Asia-Pacific Population Journal*, Vol 4, No 2, June 1989

Bajracharya, Dr. Keshar Man, "Fuelwood and Forest Loss—Burning Issue", *Rising Nepal*, 23 June 1990